SKI TEAMS

3rd in a series by

B. Briers

For

Nick, Tom and Charlie.

What fun we've had on the slopes!

My thanks go to…

Martin our favourite ski guide in the Arlberg.

All the 

design team at Chaos,

Also to Emma, for all your help.

CHAPTER 1

SNOWMAN

As told by Barney

"Barney, do you think there's a monster living on this mountain?" Our chair lift rises high above the clouds into the blue sky that stretches on forever. I look up at my big mate's round face. His goggles are misted up and I can only see one eye clearly. "I heard something about a horrible snowman that comes out after dark," says Barry. "A massive scary thing with sharp teeth."

"Ugh?" I'm trying not to laugh as I stare back across the snow-covered mountain tops poking through the fluffy cloud. Barry's so funny, he has such a great imagination.

His skis slide along the icy pathway as the chair lift reaches the top of the mountain. Whilst Barry stretches his long legs and stands up, I have to hop forward to get my skis down onto the floor. The sun is slowly sinking in the sky as I slide out of the lift station. I pull over to the side and look back for Barry as he struggles to unhook his ski poles, which are wrapped around one hand. His body rocks from side to side as he shuffles away from the chair. The poles cross and get tangled between his legs whilst he wrestles with the straps caught under the cuff of his jacket.

"Mind out!" I warn him as he bumps into me. He trips dangerously close to the edge of the mountain. His skis clatter forward but he manages to stay upright, finally freeing the poles' straps.

"Phew!" he sighs. "I thought I was going over the edge then, into the danger zone where the horrible snowman lives," he shivers.

"What are you talking about? There's no horrible snowman," I reply, distracted by Hattie, my twin sister. She's waving wildly at us across the piste. Her brown pony-tail swishing out the back of her helmet as her head flicks from looking at me to down the mountain, where skiers are disappearing into the hanging cloud.

"Some sort of ice monster…" rambles Barry.

"There's Mum and Hattie," I cut him off. "Let's go!" I head off in their direction.

I'm glad we've managed a few runs this afternoon, to get my ski legs working. I haven't skied since last year and there's a skill to zooming down a slope on a pair of thin planks. I'm cutting through the snow like a pro, but I notice Barry needs a bit more practice. He's always one wobble away from a wipeout. It's like skiing with the leaning Tower of Pisa; he just doesn't look like he's going to remain upright.

"Ready for the last run down?" Mum calls out as we slide towards her. She worked at a hotel in a ski resort for a year after leaving school. Cleaning the loos sounds grim, but it meant she got to ski every afternoon, so she's a good skier.

"Hurry up!" Hattie waves her gloved hand at us, urging us to come closer. "I've just seen Olive and her family," she squeals. "We need to go, I want to catch up with her."

Olive is Hattie's best friend, the girl with amazing fiery-red hair and a heart-shaped face. Her family is skiing in the same Austrian resort as us. They're even staying in the same hotel, along with three other families whose kids are in our year group at school. I reckon the local travel agent must have been offering a good deal on this place.

"Slow down Hattie," Mum pleads as my sister turns her skis to face down the slope. "You'll be with Olive all day tomorrow in your ski group lesson."

I pretend to fiddle with my boot clips to delay us. I want more time to practise on our own before skiing with other kids from school.

"Aw, Mum, I want to see how good she is. Please let's go."

Mum rolls her eyes then waves Hattie on, allowing her to lead the way. Barry and I follow.

"Barney, wait for me, don't leave me behind," Barry calls out as Mum and Hattie pull further away from us. This section of the piste narrows as we take a pathway curving around the mountain. I move over to the side and let him overtake me. My mate's a bit slower as he's only been skiing twice before. He had a few dry-ski slope lessons too before our holiday. I think he's a bit nervous.

Hattie picks up the pace, chasing after Olive, with Mum right behind her, and the distance between us grows. Barry's skis are bouncing over the ruts on the icy piste and his legs wobble like jelly. We dive into the cloud that hangs like a halo around the mountaintop.

"Woah!" I hear him cry. His body leans to one side and his left ski lifts up into the air. He swings his shoulders to the other side trying to rebalance but he goes too far and quickly smashes into the soft snow at the side of the piste.

"Wipeout!" I cry, hoping Mum might hear me, but her figure disappears into the fog.

I flick my skis onto their edges and pull up to collect Barry's sticks, which are strewn across the path. As I bend down to pick up one pole, a bright orange set of legs appears out of nowhere coming straight towards me.

"Watch out!" the skier shouts.

I stand up quickly and jump to the side nearly toppling over too. The skier swerves to avoid the ski pole then stops sharply just beyond it, spinning their skis around to face us uphill.

"Quick, pick the poles up! My mum and brother are on their way, you'll cause a crash Barney," the skier warns me, his face hidden by a mirrored visor on his helmet. I know the voice though.

I hurry to collect up Barry's poles.

"Ralph is that you?" I ask. The skier flicks up his visor and I recognise his face. The girls at school think he looks like a singer from a boy band, but I don't reckon he does. He glares at me. "Get the poles, hurry!"

I grab the sticks and shuffle over to where Barry's brushing snow off himself.

"This snow gets everywhere," Barry whines like a dog. "Urh, it's melting inside my jacket."

A woman in a gold helmet and a young boy dressed in green fly past us. Ralph waves his pole at them.

"Right, I'm off," he says. "Don't want to be the last on the mountain, not with the Abominable Snowman waking up off piste."

"What are you talking about?" I sneer.

"Then again, I can see you're obviously not good enough to be going off piste." Ralph looks down at Barry still sitting in the snow. "You might survive if you get down before it's dark."

Ralph jumps on his skis and zips off into the fog. Barry grabs the poles from me, digs them in the ground and quickly pushes himself up.

"Is that a snowman that eats people?" he checks with me.

"I've no idea. He's just making it up," I grumble, still staring at the place where the orange legs were last seen. "How dare he say I'm not good enough to ski off piste. He hasn't even seen me ski yet. What does he know anyway?"

Barry is fiddling with his gloves. "I don't think we should hang around too long up here though," he says, pinging his goggles back down onto his face. "It's spooky on our own."

A sudden gust of icy wind whips around the bend, carrying a moaning howl.

"What was that?" We both instinctively spin to face the wind. The freezing blast catches our breath. That howl is creepy.

"It's the… it's the… it's the horrible snowman!" cries Barry.

"Let's go!" I shout, digging my sticks into the ground and poling away as fast as possible. Barry gallops on his skis beside me. We pick up speed, slicing through the fog. I keep hearing the moaning in my head. I crouch down to go faster, Barry copies me. Neither one of us wants to be at the back. My leg muscles are cramping up, I'm trying so hard to hold my skis steady. The slope drops sharply, my skis leave the snow for a second, and my stomach jumps until my skis smash back down onto the snow. Just as Barry's weight carries him ahead, we shoot out of the cloud, into the clear. I spy two figures waiting to one side. I've never been so glad to see my sister.

"We wondered where you two had got to?" Mum says as we rush towards them.

"We were about to send out a search party," jokes Hattie.

Barry and I brake sharply, both of us breathing heavily.

"Everything all right?" Mum asks. My parents are acting as Barry's guardians on the trip since his mum didn't want to come. She's not a skier like my mum. Barry told me that this ski trip is both his birthday and Christmas present.

I glance at Barry. He's looking back up the mountain into the fog. The wind has died. More people drop out of the cloud and ski past us.

"Yeah, fine," I lie. "Barry took a tumble, that's all."

"Oh Barry I am sorry, I didn't realise, otherwise I would've stopped to help. Are you ok?" Mum apologises but Barry's got other things on his mind.

"We'd better head in now that the chair lifts are stopping," he answers, no doubt eager to get back to the safety of the hotel. In the distance I can just see the top of the wooden-clad building sitting at the base of the slope, its roof covered in a deep layer of snow like a giant pillow. He takes one last worried look up the mountain.

"Yes of course," Mum agrees.

Barry is already gliding away so I follow. He doesn't want to be last and neither do I.

***

In the dim light of the hotel lounge this evening, together with the other kids from school, we huddle around a table in the corner playing cards.

I'm sat between Vijay and Barry. Vijay's a mate of mine, a small, incredibly clever guy. I like to sit next to him in maths because he knows all the answers. The three girls, Hattie, Olive and Eve are sat the other side of the table. Eve's always smiling and hasn't been at our school that long. She's in my English class and can quote the alphabet backwards in three different languages. At the head of the table sits Ralph, he's already thirteen, the oldest in our year, and he makes sure everyone knows it. I don't have any classes with him but I've heard he can be a big head. I've never forgiven him for tripping me up in the 800 metres race on sports day in our first year. He claims it was an accident but he went on to win and I came last. It was obviously tactical, he must've seen me as a threat. Maybe that's why he joked about my skiing earlier.

A blizzard spins outside the window. Ralph is taking over, as I expected he would. Reckons he's got something scary to tell us now that the parents have gone off to the bar.

"At the top of the highest cable car at the side of the steepest black run is where the creature lives. It waits until dusk, when the mist covers the mountain and the icy wind blasts the peak. That's when it treks out of the hidden cave to hunt down its victims." Ralph purses his lips, whistling like the wind through the cracks in the window frame.

Barry's pinkie finger prods the back of my hand.

"He's making it up," I whisper in his ear, but my mate's eyes are glued to the storyteller.

Putting his fingers onto the top card in the pack, Ralph slides the card forward.

"The Ace of Snowman," he hisses, suddenly flipping the card over to reveal the scariest snowman. No carrot for a nose on this one, instead a mouth packed with sharp icicles for teeth, and icy-blue-and-red-veined eyes that glare at you from every direction. Where did that come from? I don't remember that card being in the pack before. I shuffle sideways on my seat yet the eyes still seem to be watching me.

Hattie chews on her fingernails and Olive shrinks down into her polo neck jumper, her chin disappearing beneath the wool.

"Last skiers down the mountain are in grave danger," Ralph warns, just like he told us earlier this afternoon. "No one that lives has ever seen it, but many speak of the gigantic footprints left behind after a treacherous night of blizzards. Some say it leaves the bones of its last dinner spat out amongst the trees."

Olive squeaks like a mouse. The girls shuffle a little closer to one another, glancing nervously out of the window into the night. The snow is falling so fast that they've stopped clearing the road. Snowflakes swirl in the wind, one minute flying sideways then spinning like a twister the next.

I slouch back in my chair. He's talking rubbish, I tell myself.

"Don't stay out alone after dark on the mountain when the weather is bad, that's what the elders of the village say." He points to a faded black and white photo on the wall. It's of a group of old men on skis, wearing jackets and brimmed hats. They look ancient. Ralph's voice is barely a whisper now. Everyone leans in closer, gripped by his story. I only sit forward in order to hear. "First you'll feel the cold and you'll be disorientated by the swirling snow, not knowing which way to go. You'll have the feeling that you're being followed."

Barry shudders next to me. I raise an eyebrow at him, but he's hypnotised, concentrating on the tale spewing from Ralph's lips.

"And in the deep, heavy snowfall, if the Abominable Snowman is waiting for you…" Ralph's voice is rising up to the climax, "…you'll be lucky to survive!" he booms.

Hattie and Olive squeal, clutching each other. Barry sinks down, pulling his bobble hat over his ears.

"Vijay!" I push my mate's bony body away from me as he tries to jump onto my lap.

Eve rolls her eyes. "I've heard it all before Ralph, you and your ridiculous stories," she says.

Eve's the only one not shaking, apart from me of course. She pokes Ralph with one of her crutches and he flinches. Eve's left leg was amputated below the knee when she was very young. Tonight her leg is sore from rubbing on her prosthetic limb so she chose not to wear it. Instead of walking into the bar she came in on crutches, her left trouser leg folded up below the knee. Her crutches are cool, covered in stickers she's collected at ski shows over the years.

"Yeah, Ralph," I mock. "Just coz you've been here loads of times before, you're trying to scare us all."

Ralph sits back and folds his arms.

"Well if you don't want to believe me Barney, that's up to you." He stands up, collecting up the pack of cards off the table. Ralph won every game of trumps tonight. "I guess you're not good enough to be left out on the mountain on your own anyway. There'll always be someone there to hold your hand," he smirks. "Let's hope your skiing's better than your card playing!"

The girls giggle, even my sister, who should stick up for me. I squash my chin into my neck and give him a death stare. I'm not a baby, I don't need anyone to hold my hand. And it wasn't my fault I came last in cards, we were playing a game I didn't know. Anyway I reckon he was cheating.

"Good night all," he says, "don't go having nightmares." Ralph hangs his hands either side of his face pretending to haunt Hattie. "Woooo!"

"Stop it!" she giggles, pushing him away.

"Good night," Ralph grins, waving as he backs out of the lounge. "Wooo!" We hear as he disappears.

All the girls are laughing. Vijay and Barry don't speak. My top lip curls, I want to growl like a dog.

Ralph's family is staying in the best suite in the hotel. Apparently it has a Jacuzzi bath, an enormous flat-screen TV and a large balcony overlooking the mountain. And they've each been given complimentary bathrobes and slippers. Our rooms are at the back of the hotel overlooking the car park. I'm sharing a small twin room with Barry and we're in bunk beds. I'm not sure the bed could hold Barry's long body on the top bunk as his feet hang out over the end. Luckily he's agreed to go on the bottom bed. Hattie's got a camp bed in my parents' room. I think Olive's family has a suite of rooms too, but she doesn't boast about it like Ralph does.

Dad wanders over.

"Come on kids, we're all going to bed now. We've got an early start in the morning." He cups his hands around his face and presses against the window, his hot breath steaming up a patch on the glass. "Looks like the snow will be good," he says. "Ooh, I wouldn't want to be out there tonight. Good job we're not camping out eh Barney?" He looks back and nudges me with his elbow.

Camping? Nobody camps in a ski resort. I don't engage. Dad is so embarrassing.

"Aren't you hot?" I ask Barry who's insisted on wearing his woolly bobble hat ever since we got off the plane.

Barry sits up, folding the bottom of his hat back up above his ears.

"No, it's snowing Barney, why would I be hot?"

"We're inside," I point out.

"Yeah, lucky that, coz we wouldn't want to be camping outside like your Dad says." Barry lowers his voice and leans across to my ear. "Not with the horrible snowman."

"I think I see something flashing on the mountain," says Dad.

"What? Where?" Hattie and Olive jump to window, peering into the dark.

"I hope it's not the abdominal snowman," grunts Barry.

"Abominable not abdominal!" Vijay shakes his head.

"Could be some sort of monster? Big bright eyes," Dad declares, "menacing and flashing."

"It's a snow plough!" Olive chuckles. "It's bashing the slopes."

"Forgive me Olive, this skiing lark is all new to me I'm afraid. I've only been on a pair of skis once, and that was a long time ago," Dad explains.

I slap my forehead and cover my eyes. Is he going to be like this all week?

"Phew!" says Barry, pulling his hat off. "I thought we were in trouble then."

"Ralph's making it up Barry," I tell him. I don't believe anything Ralph said this evening, especially after he questioned my skiing skills. I reckon off piste can't be much more difficult. I'll show him how good I am.

CHAPTER 2

SKI GEAR

As told by Barney

What's electric blue with yellow lightning strips? Sadly, the answer is my dad's all-in-one ski suit. It's so old fashioned and looks more like fancy dress for a 1980's disco.

"You're not wearing that are you?" I check, blocking his exit from the bedroom.

"Hasn't this lasted me well?" He strokes the fabric on the sleeve. "Flash isn't it?"

I stare at him, horrified at the thought of us being seen together in public.

"Still fits after all these years." He tugs at the front zip as he tries to pull it up past his thermal top. The fabric is pulling so tight across his belly that he has to draw in a deep breath before the zip will budge. Quickly, he yanks the zip up to the top. "Ooh, it's cosy."

Too tight in other words.

Barry walks up behind me. My friend's wearing a red jacket and black salopettes that he's borrowed from his cousin. He stops at Dad's doorway, his eyes widening at the sight of the shiny fabric.

"Morning Barry, you ready for our first full day of skiing?" Dad asks him.

Barry squints, quietly pulling his goggles down over his eyes. "Yeah, are you?" Barry asks politely. He's obviously not seen anything like Dad's suit before.

Mum pops her head up over Dad's shoulder. "Hi boys."

She squeezes past the electric blue suit. Her outfit is much more subtle, a black jacket with a red stripe down the arms and red salopettes. Mum skied a lot with Grandpa when she was younger and she's taken Hattie and me on her own twice before. This is the first time I've been on a ski holiday with Dad. And if he insists on wearing such embarrassing kit, I may well refuse to go with him in the future.

"Shall we go and get our skis and boots?" she suggests, walking off down the corridor. Hattie nips past Dad, her head down avoiding eye contact, and quickly follows Mum. She's also wearing a black jacket but with luminous yellow salopettes, a christmas present from Grandpa. They're bright but pretty cool, unlike Dad's shiny suit.

Dad steps out, pulling the door closed behind him. He stands with one shiny electric blue leg next to mine.

"Blue trousers," he says pointing down to our legs, "we're nearly matching."

He marches off, leaving me staring at my matt blue legs.

"Please tell me I look nothing like my dad."

Barry takes off his goggles. "At least he'll be easy to spot on the mountain." We laugh.

***

The boot room is packed full of people tugging on heavy buckled boots and big helmets. The trick is to get your boots on first, your helmet next, followed by goggles and gloves, then make a quick exit with your skis and poles before you overheat in the crowded room. Hattie and Mum get out first, followed by Barry and me, but there's no sign of Dad.

"Let's walk over to the ski school. I told your father we'd wait for him there," says Mum.

I carry my skis on one shoulder and trudge through the snow to where a crowd of people stands. Amongst them I spy Olive in a pair of yellow salopettes and a black jacket just like Hattie. Looks like they're a team and I'm sure they must have planned it. Though Olive's got bright yellow goggles too. I reckon they glow in the dark. Eve is wearing the reverse, bright green jacket and black leggings and a green backpack to match. Vijay's all in dark blue with yellow stripes down the side of his legs.

As I reach the others, I spy the pair of orange salopettes flying down to the bottom of the piste. The boy stops close by, spraying me and Barry with snow. He laughs but I don't.

"Oi!" Barry shouts, brushing the snow off his legs.

"Ralph, stop showing off," Eve scolds him. She slides over to us on her skis.

"Hey Ralph, did you buy those skis coz the orange stripes match your trousers?" Barry asks. Ralph grins but doesn't answer. "We hired our skis didn't we Barney?"

I pull my skis apart and let each one drop onto the snow.

"The horrible snowman," blurts Barry, hanging his head over my skis. "I knew I'd seen those eyes somewhere before." He points to the pattern drawn on my skis.

Vijay peers over his poles. "Exactly the same as on the cards last night." He shivers.

"What if the Abdominal Snowman legend is true?" asks Barry.

I'm about to say, 'don't be daft', when Vijay interrupts.

"Abominable not Abdominal. Your abdomen is the part of the body between your head and your legs," Vijay corrects him.

"That's probably the part of you he eats first," Barry suggests.

"We're with that instructor over there," Eve butts in, directing Ralph to a small group wearing backpacks at the base of another chair lift. "Come on, they're waiting for us. See you later guys." Eve digs her poles into the snow, pushing herself towards her group. Thankfully this distracts everyone from the discussion about my skis.

Eve's been skiing here since she was four. She told me that her group instructor is the man who originally taught her to ski years before. When Eve was seven, her family moved abroad for two years and lived close to these mountains. They would come skiing with the same instructor every weekend. I bet she's really good.

Before Ralph leaves, a tall man stops abruptly beside him. The gentleman Is dressed all in black with a black visor on his black helmet.

"He looks like a secret assassin," whispers Barry.

"I'm going with your mother to find Hugo's private instructor." I hear him say in a very posh voice like someone's pinched his nose. He waves at a gold helmet zigzagging down the slope followed by Ralph's little brother dressed all in green like a giant frog bombing along behind. "We will meet you back in the suite this afternoon," he instructs Ralph. Not waiting for his son to reply, the man glides away, using his skis like a pair of skates.

"That's cool," Barry mumbles beside me. "How does he do that? I can't do that, can you?"

"Err, yeah, ish," I pretend.

Ralph overhears. "Can't wait to see how good you are at skiing off piste Barney."

I've never been off piste but I'm not going to admit that to him. I wish I could think of something funny to reply and make him look silly. I ignore him. Besides, people are turning away, more interested in a commotion back at the entrance to the ski shop under our hotel. Some of my friends start laughing.

"That guy took the head off the mannequin by the shop door as he swung his skis over his shoulder," one English boy says pointing.

I look back to see an assistant rushing out to rescue the toppled body of the mannequin from the snow. Another person collects up the model's head and offers it back to the assistant. Whilst the mannequin is being reassembled, the skier who caused the problem is struggling to control the long skis in his arms as they cross and slide about. Waving from the straps around his wrists, his poles are threatening to whip anyone who gets too close.

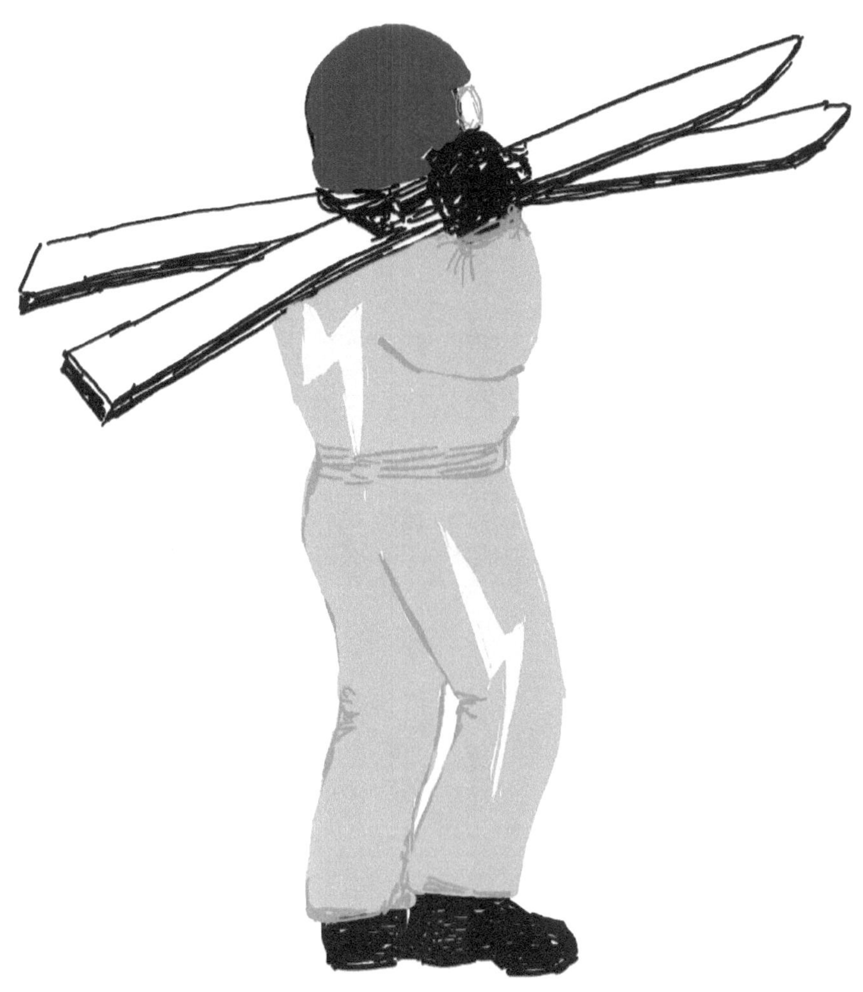

"What a joker!" sneers Ralph. "A danger to the slopes."
Shaking his head, Ralph sidesteps away and goes in search
of his group.

I bite my lip.

"He's so embarrassing," Hattie mumbles, holding a glove
across her mouth.

"I think he needs a bit of help," Mum smiles. She puts down her skis and plants her poles in the snow before walking across to Dad.

"He's so funny," laughs Vijay.

"And so bright in that suit with the lightning flashes," Hattie mocks, puffing out her cheeks.

"We should call him 'Lightning Flash'," Vijay suggests. Everyone laughs except me.

I thump my poles into the snow and lean heavily on them.

"Why does he have to be my dad?" I sigh.

The blue-and-red-veined eyes glare back at me.

CHAPTER 3

FIRST LESSON

As told by Barney

"Look through the window down to the valley," drills Christophe our guide in his foreign accent. He's trying to improve our parallel turns. Holding his arms out straight in front, pointing his poles up to the sky to create 'a window', he slides across the run. "Hips to the mountain Barney, body down to the valley. Push forward over the tips of your skis. That's good Olive. Keep your skis parallel Vijay! No snowplough Barry! Barry!"

I glance up to see the red jacket shooting off across the piste.

"Lean forward, down to the valley!" Christophe instructs.

Barry leans back and his skis move even faster, bouncing over bumps. Poles wave uncontrollably in the air as he careers across the piste, narrowly missing another skier racing downhill. Christophe jumps into action, flying after his student.

But the boy is beyond help, his legs begin to wobble, he catches an edge and one ski skids off at an angle breaking free from the boot binding. Left with only one ski, Barry topples onto his backside in the snow as his other ski shoots off down the hill.

Christophe reaches his pupil and checks, "Barry are you OK? All your legs and arms still in one piece?"

Clad in a layer of snow, Barry's head and body rise from the ground. He leans on his elbows.

"It's the Abdominal Snowman!" Vijay jokes.

We're all in hysterics. Barry's wipeouts are becoming legendary. He's already taken out our instructor once this morning.

Meanwhile, a fast stylish skier cruises by and collects up Barry's stray ski. The man clambers back up the piste to return the ski to its owner. Barry's face is agog. He doesn't get up for a bit. Instead he stares after the ski rescuer, who glides away down the run, like a snake slithering through the snow.

"Did you see him?" Barry asks as he rejoins the group.

"Who?"

"The secret assassin," he says, pulling at his goggles and wiping away a chunk of snow wedged under his helmet.

"Oh him," I try to act disinterested.

"He's amazing," Barry drones.

"Perhaps it's best we try a different exercise," says Christophe.

Trust Ralph's dad to be so cool.

***

The morning lesson flies by. We all manage to remember how to ski, some better than others. Christophe calls us 'The Crazy Team'. Olive's pretty good. She should be in the group above us but she wants to be with Hattie. Vijay takes his time and is often at the back, but he's very precise about his technique. There's another boy called Oscar who's fallen over nearly as many times as Barry. Oscar thinks he knows what he's doing and tries to go faster than anyone else. We're supposed to follow Christophe in a line weaving our way down the mountain, taking it in turns to be at the front. Oscar keeps overtaking on the turns by taking shortcuts, claiming he's out of control or we're going too slowly. Either way he always ends up right behind the instructor.

Barry thinks he's the worst in the group. He suffers from a big lack of confidence only outweighed by his mad desire for adventure. He overtakes people by complete accident, usually just before his legs give way, causing a multiple pile up of skiers.

"My legs are tired," he moans after our first day of skiing. "Look at them shaking." He plonks himself down on the bench in the ski shop and starts to remove his boots.

"My legs are shaking with fear every time you're anywhere near me," says Vijay. "You're a liability. I think that's why the instructor calls us the Crazy Team." Vijay's boots are already off, buckled up and stacked on the shelf.

"You need to lie in a hot bath. That's what I'm going to do," Olive tells him.

"Poo! You definitely need a bath coz your feet stink!" claims Hattie wafting a hand under her nose as Barry yanks off one of his boots.

"A bath! What does he want a bath for?" I sneer. What a waste of time. We've got more important things to do like practise playing cards. I'm not losing to Ralph again this evening. Pity our instructor didn't talk about going off piste, I'll need some help in case I decide to challenge Ralph to a race later in the week. I'm sure deep snow can't be much more difficult than skiing on the piste. If anything it'll be a softer landing.

"Wish we had a jacuzzi bath like Ralph, don't you Barney?" Barry elbows me.

"Not really." I try to ignore him by busying myself with pulling off my boots.

"I wonder if Ralph was in ski school all day? His group is probably The Top Team. Or maybe he went skiing with the secret assassin this afternoon," he waffles on.

"Yeah they probably went heli-skiing," I sneer. That is the most expensive way to get dropped at the top of a mountain, by helicopter.

"Wow, do you think they did?" Barry drones on. "That'd be amazing. But it'd mean they'd be in that off piste part where the Ab…, Abd…, horrible snowman lives. Dicing with danger." His big eyes nearly pop out.

Turning away from my mate, I screw my face up. I feel all hot and bothered. Hattie catches me. She raises her eyebrows but I don't respond. Instead I get up, stomp across the room and stuff my boots onto the shelf.

"You going already?" Barry whines as I pick up my helmet and gloves. "Wait for me." He scoops up his boots and jogs over to the shelves.

I'm already walking out to the lift.

***

"Owww!" Dad howls as Mum struggles to release him from the all-in-one suit. Finally, he lies flaked out on the bed in just his Union Jack thermals.

"What's the matter with Dad?" I ask. I only popped in for the Wi-Fi code.

"He's a bit sore after his first day," Mum kindly explains.

"Yeah, it must be tough in the beginners group and being overtaken by a bunch of five year olds!" my sister teases him.

"Very funny Hattie," Dad replies. He's not laughing. "I'll have you know that snowplough is extremely tough on the old thighs." Dad tries to roll onto his side. "Aarh! Can somebody run me a bath?"

"Where did you go Mum?" I ask.

"I teamed up with Ralph's mum as she was on her own," I feel my shoulders flop, "and some of the other parents too. What a lovely lady." I notice Hattie looks up from the book she's reading. "Her outfit is so chic. I think her husband was off doing some daringly difficult run."

"I'll probably join him later in the week," Dad groans as he pushes his body up from the bed and limps towards the bathroom. "I'll run my own bath since no one's offering to run one for me." Dad stands in the doorway, his bottom lip drooping as he tries to look hurt.

"His dad's a really good skier," Hattie butts in, her eyes widening. "Isn't he Barney?" I shrug, hanging my head down. "I bet Ralph's good too. Did you see him this morning? He was wearing this off piste rucksack kit. Olive and I were talking about it over lunch."

"I expect you'll be as good as him by the end of the week," I nod to Dad and he smiles back.

Someone's got to stick up for Dad.

CHAPTER 4

SNOW KING

As told by Barney

Four cards are dealt from the pack in a cross shape onto the table. All seven of us from school are sat together in the lounge. I brought my own pack down tonight, in case Ralph's snowman cards are marked and that's how he cheats.

"The game is called Kings," Ralph announces

"Aren't we playing with your snowman cards tonight with that scary joker card?" Olive asks Ralph. "We could play the game of the Abominable Snowman!"

Ralph grins at her. "It's probably easier to explain using these ordinary cards."

They're not ordinary cards, they're a pack that Grandpa gave me.

A red seven, a black queen, a red four and a black ten lie on the table. With the rest of the pack, Vijay deals seven cards out to every player. Ralph demonstrates how to play by laying a black six from his hand on top of the red seven.

"You can only place the next lower number down and it has to be the opposite colour," he explains. "So you could put a red nine on the black ten, or a red jack on the black queen."

"Now I can put a red five on your black six," says Vijay, pulling cards from his hand, eager to play.

"Yes, but it's not your go," Ralph puts his arm out to stop Vijay placing the cards down. "We play clockwise from the dealer." Ralph circles his pointy finger around the group. "Olive it's your go next."

"But that means I go last but one," moans Vijay.

"Olive, you're first," Ralph indicates, ignoring Vijay.

She sits up, shaking her mane of wavy hair that must keep her ears warm in cold weather. For a minute she stares at her cards, fanning them out in her hand. Then she looks at the cards on the table and back to her hand again. Sensing her hesitation, Ralph offers some guidance.

"Do you have a red nine?" he asks, pointing to the black ten.

"No," Olive replies.

"How about a black three?" Ralph's finger moves across to the red four.

"No."

"A red jack?" He doesn't bother pointing at the cards this time. Olive shakes her head. "Or a red five?"

"I have a red five," announces Vijay once again.

"Yes, I know that, but it's not your go," Ralph clips his words.

"How about a king, any king?" he asks.

"Yes, I've got the king of diamonds." Olive plucks the card out of her hand to show the group.

Ralph takes the card from her and places it in the corner between the queen and the seven.

"Kings can start a new pile to collect all their own suit in descending order. Do you have the queen of diamonds or another king?" he asks Olive. She shakes her head. "Right, now it's Eve's go."

Eve puts down a five of diamonds. Vijay's nostrils flare like a bull ready to charge.

"Sorry Vijay," says Eve having taken the space for his red five. Vijay shuffles his bony body. It's difficult to remain angry with Eve, she's too nice. She selects another card from her hand, laying down a four of clubs on the red five, at which point Barry starts to bounce about on the seat next to me, flicking one of his cards with his finger.

"Are you finished?" Ralph asks her. Eve nods. "Barney," Ralph prompts me.

"I can't go," I grumble.

"Pick up a card from the pile in that case."

I pick up a king. I smile immediately and go to place the king into one of the corners like Ralph explained. I've already got the queen of the same suit too.

"Not yet," Ralph pushes my hand away. "You'll have to wait for your next turn."

I slump back into the chair. At least I'll be able to play two cards next time."

"My go," Barry reaches forwards to slap down a three of diamonds.

"Very good," Ralph praises him.

"I like this game," says Barry.

"Is it finally my go?" Vijay asks.

Ralph nods.

Vijay rests his elbows on the table, rubbing his forefinger against his nose. He's concentrating; we all sit quietly waiting. His forefinger slides back and forth across the tops of his fanned out cards. Finally stopping on the penultimate card in his hand, he pinches the corner between his thumb and finger. He starts mumbling, his mouth and nose twitching. We all wait patiently.

"No," he eventually decides, "I can't go." He reaches over to collect a card from the pile.

"Hattie's turn." Ralph slips back in his chair and looks over Hattie's shoulder. "I'll help you," he says quietly.

Hattie's shoulders wriggle and she leans towards Ralph showing him her hand. My sister points to one of her cards, tilting her head to look up at her helper.

"Yes, go ahead," Ralph quietly encourages her.

She places the king of clubs in the corner.

"Now let me show you. Hattie can take the queen of clubs off the cross and put it on top of the king," Ralph moves it for her, "now she can place one of her own cards in the space left."

Hattie selects a card and shows Ralph, but he shakes his head and whispers into her ear, touching the tops of a few other cards in her hand.

"Oh yeah," she sighs. My sister's gone all shy and is fluttering her eyelashes at Ralph, it's weird. She places a red nine in the space on the cross.

"Couldn't she have put that on the black ten?" Vijay questions. He's really got the hang of this game.

Ralph and Hattie look at each other and smile. He gives her another encouraging nod.

"I haven't finished yet Vijay," Hattie informs him.

She pulls another card from her hand, the jack of clubs, and places it down on top of the queen in the corner. Then she picks up the black ten moving it across to the jack. This leaves another free space on the cross, where she lays a black five. Swiftly picking up the red four, she transfers it onto the black five and then slaps down a black eight from her hand.

"Finally!" Olive huffs, leaning forward to take a turn.

"No, no, no," Ralph waves a hand at Olive, who freezes, holding her card in mid air. Ralph signals to Hattie, his eyes darting back and forth between the cards and Hattie's hand now holding just two cards.

My sister stares at the cards on the table and then back at her hand. It's blindingly obvious that the red seven can go onto the black eight and then the whole pile can be moved onto the red nine.

"She's had enough time, let someone else have a go," I complain.

"Patience Barney, it's your sister's first game." Ralph reprimands me so calmly it's like an adult scolding a child. I feel silly.

"I've got it!" cries Hattie as she realises the move.

She collects up the red seven and all the cards on top if it, moves the pile across to the black eight and then onto the red nine, leaving two empty spaces on the cross. She lays down a ten of diamonds in the empty space. With a pathetic smile, she then shows her last card to her extremely helpful assistant.

"I've forgotten, do I put this in the corner?" she asks him.

"No, no." He takes the card from her hand, and with a big cheesy grin, places the queen of hearts on the last remaining space and announces, "Hattie's the winner, the Snow King!"

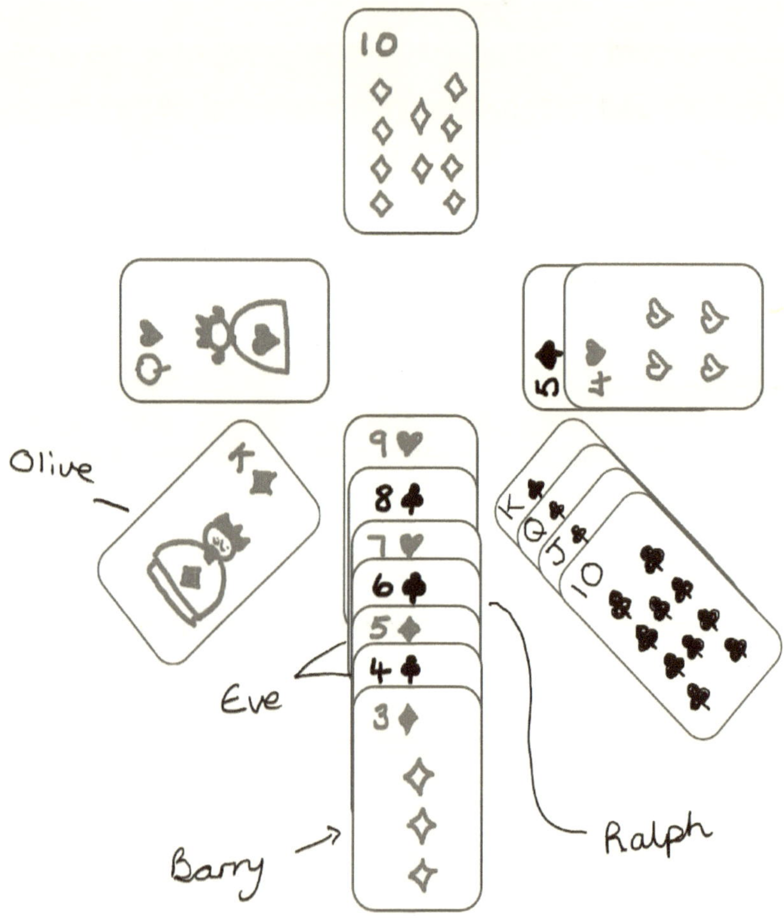

Hattie cups her reddening cheeks with her hands.

"Can we play again so that we can all get a go this time?" Vijay starts collecting up the cards and shuffling. "I'll go first this time," he says.

"Stupid game if you ask me," I mumble, but nobody's listening, they're all too busy checking the rules with Ralph.

***

When I get back to the room, I decide to send an email to Grandpa. I promised to keep him updated throughout the holiday. Shame he wasn't able to come, but at least he's got Clyde the kitten for company back home.

Hi Grandpa. We've arrived. Been skiing with our instructor. Thankfully I can remember how to ski. Barry needs a bit more help. We'll have a go at a black run soon, and maybe some deep snow off the side of the piste.

Playing cards with friends every evening. I lost ☹ and Hattie won but she had help from Ralph, a boy from school, he's a bit annoying.

Got to take Dad up on the chair lift tomorrow for the first time ever! He's nowhere near as good as you and Mum at skiing. Don't think he'll be going on any black runs.

Wish you were here. Love Barney

PS: Hope Clyde hasn't pooed on the kitchen floor again.

CHAPTER 5

CHAIR LIFT

As told by Barney

Every step is an effort. It's like walking with a snail. "Come on Dad, I'll be late for my lesson if you don't hurry up." The trip from the ski shop to the bottom of the lift has never taken me so long.

"You've no idea how sore I am Barney," groans Dad.

When I look at him, all I can see is his electric blue suit straining with the effort of holding in his stomach.

"I think it's because I've got such big muscles. I must produce more lactic acid than wimps. That's why it hurts me more," Dad professes.

I'm not sure that being a wimp has much to do with muscle size. Surely even the skinniest person can be brave and the biggest muscly person can still be scared of spiders? It's not worth explaining to Dad. I trudge on carrying Dad's skis as well as my own, whilst all he carries is our poles.

"I'll meet you at the lift Dad." I give up on being slow.

"Alright son," he puffs, his hot breath forming clouds in the cold morning air.

It's Dad's first day on the chair lift today, having spent the first few days on the magic carpet with the five year olds. Mum and I said we'd wait for him and we could all travel up together. Adult skiers are often asked to help take small children up on the lifts but today I'll be helping to take up Dad. Hattie's gone on ahead with Olive to meet our instructor at the top. She says it's too embarrassing to be seen with Dad. I think that's unfair, as everyone has to learn sometime, but I agree he could at least be less conspicuous by wearing a different outfit.

I just don't get it, why is Dad so rubbish at skiing? He used to be good at football, he can pass a rugby ball straight when playing in the garden with me and Hattie. He even calls himself a sportsman. So, how come he's not good at every sport?

Finally Dad trudges up to join Mum and me in the queue.

"Clean mountain air!" he sings, drawing in a deep breath, probably to mask the fact that he's out of breath. He was puffing hard as he arrived. I reckon he should have done some training before coming on this holiday. More exercise than just walking from the front door to the car and back everyday.

We spend five minutes bashing all the snow off his boots before we secure his first foot into the ski binding. He wobbles over, planting the other foot in fresh snow. The leg that's already attached to a ski swings wildly in the air, nearly bashing the knee caps of a very smart fur-clad woman. She spits a mouthful of foreign words at him. Dad raises his eyebrows; he's got no idea what she's saying. Mum jumps in to try and calm the situation.

"Enscholegon," Mum apologises in her best accent. I know that word, it means sorry or excuse me.

We pull Dad up and he tries to kick his other boot into a snow-covered ski. People down the queue are staring and grunting, probably wondering why we aren't moving forward.

"Barney!" Eve waves to me from further down the line. She stands amongst the Top Team, which includes Ralph. They've probably done one run already. I manage a weak smile back. I wish she hadn't noticed me. Mum signals to a few people to go ahead of us, including the rest of Dad's group, while we try to sort him out. The instructor waits behind. I'm glad as I think we might need help with Dad. Skiing obviously isn't his sport.

"So you boys are going on a black run with Christophe this morning," the instructor says as he clears snow from Dad's ski. All the instructors speak English which is helpful since my German isn't that good.

"Yeah, can't wait," replies Barry.

"How about a black run for you today?" The instructor looks at Dad whose lips twitch but don't speak. "Only joking!" He slaps Dad on the back before ramming his boot into the ski. "You are ready! Let's go."

Finally clipped in, we edge forward, shuffling our skis along the path as we line up for the lift. Mum stands on the far side, waiting at the barrier. Barry stands to my right and Dad is to my left, sandwiched between Mum and me. We are taking the next chair and the instructor will be on the one behind.

We watch the chair ahead of us, scooping up the skiers waiting in front. The barriers lift and we edge forward. All except Dad, who hesitates. Mum and I quickly reach back, just managing to grab his arms and drag him forward.

"I didn't realise you had to do that," he says. He's a bit flustered and is fiddling about with his poles and gloves, not concentrating on what's going on at all.

The chair lift bangs into my calf then we're thrown back onto the chair.

"We're in," I mutter, turning to Barry as the chair lift moves us slowly through the station. "Now we've just got to get him off the other…"

"What are you doing?" Mum shrieks.

I spin back to see her trying to grab at Dad's suit as he tumbles forward onto the icy path. Her mittens slip off the shiny material.

"I dropped my glove…ow!" Dad and his voice disappear beneath the chair just as the safety bar comes down to prevent us all from falling off. Alarm bells start ringing and the lift slows down and stops with us suspended a few metres up in the air. Rip! We look back to see Dad bent over in a heap, his electric blue suit ripped at the seam across his bottom, exposing his Union Jack thermals.

"Oh dear, that's a serious suit malfunction," says Mum biting her lip, trying hard not to laugh.

"It's a bit embarrassing," Barry sniggers.

A bit! That's an understatement. I hide my face in my gloves.

The instructor jumps the barriers to go to Dad's rescue. "I think you need to go shopping for a new suit," I hear him say. He unclips Dad's ski bindings so that Dad can stand up. They are laughing. I suppose I should be grateful that he wasn't hurt.

One of the lift operators guides Dad down an exit path from the lift, and the chair starts moving again. I hope Eve and the Top Team didn't see, particularly Ralph.

CHAPTER 6

BLACK RUN

As told by Barney

A cold wind picks up as I head into the clouds. This drag lift is so steep, and my legs are sore after the flight of runs we've just completed. I grip my thighs, desperate to keep my skis straight. I don't want to fall off and be stranded here alone. The Crazy Team has left the crowds on the blue and red runs, where the snow sparkles in the morning sun. We're venturing to another side of the mountain, the colder, harsh north face, where it's so quiet it's spooky. I bet this is where the Abominable Snowman lives. I scour the off piste for signs of giant footprints.

By the time I reach the top, my legs are shaking. High winds have blown the snow into ice sculptures lining the route, like a batch of misshapen meringues. A jagged rock points out of the mountain above me, its side too steep to hold the white powder. Our group huddles together like sheep, standing in silence, waiting for each member to arrive out of the cloud. Mist blows away until the peaks of the mountains are bathed in sunshine, but an arctic wind stops it from being warm. I side step to the lip of the piste and peer down. The slope drops away sharply at the top as if a section has been sliced off by a giant sword. Further down I can just make out some large bumps carved into the snow, before the piste disappears into the cloud that cloaks the top of the mountain.

"I reckon that's at least a 60 degree angle," Vijay calculates beside me.

"60, no way!" I gulp. There are warning signs flashing in my head. Get a grip Barney, you've done black runs before. You've got this covered, I tell myself.

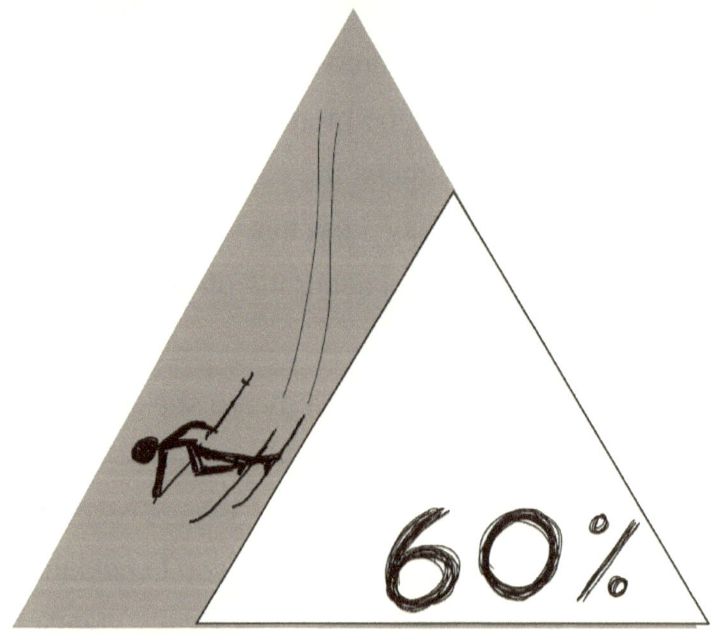

"It's not the steepest black run here either," he warns me.

Vijay's not boosting my confidence.

"At least we get a soft landing in that cloud," Barry suggests. Surely he can't seriously think that.

"OK Crazy Team," Christophe arrives following the last member of the group. "Are we ready?" he warbles, as if we are about to go on a ride at the fair. "Our first black run. Are you excited?" he asks, jumping on his skis.

A strong gust blows through the group making Olive's hair dance wildly in the wind. Vijay shivers next to me. I flinch, if we stand here much longer I think my nose might drop off, it's so cold.

"Yeah!" booms Barry. He's the only one who appears excited.

Hattie's face is hidden, masked by a scarf and her white goggles. Olive, stood beside her, nods just the once.

"Follow my lead down the slope. No overtaking." We all look at Oscar, but he ignores us. "Remember to bend your knees, lean your hips into the mountain and shift your weight onto your downhill ski." Christophe demonstrates, his skis digging into the snow on the inside edge so that the downward edge sticks out, off the ground. He slides away from us across the snow. "When you make a turn, you lift up and forward down the mountain." He straightens his legs, lurching forward, his skis flatten onto the piste and curve through the snow until he's facing towards us once more. Bending his knees back down, his edges lift up and he slides back to the group.

He makes it look so easy.

"We are going to make our way around the mounds, using them as a spot to turn upon."

How about we just avoid them altogether sounds like a better idea to me.

"Let's go! Follow me, take your time." He skis away.

For a moment no one makes a move, until there's a sudden rush by both Hattie and Olive.

"I'm going to copy exactly what he does," says Olive, pushing off first.

"Me too," mumbles Hattie from beneath her scarf, racing after her friend.

"You go first Barney," Barry suggests. "I'll follow you."

"Why don't I follow you?" I offer, my voice sounds feeble.

"You're better than me and you can catch me if I fall."

"But you're heavier than me and you'll overtake me," I argue in a deep voice, trying to sound more confident than I feel.

"No I won't, promise," Barry pauses.

Whilst we waste time discussing it, Vijay poles after the girls, along with the rest of our group. Mist rolls across the mountain and surrounds us. Suddenly Barry and I are left alone. I catch a glimpse of the eyes on my skis.

"Quick," I panic, "we need to go!" Simultaneously we dig our poles in, following the others' tracks to find the disappearing figures.

For a few seconds we seem to be skiing blind, unable to see what's ahead but feeling the bumps that pepper the piste beneath our skis. It makes me feel a bit sick.

I bend my knees hoping to feel more in control. Luckily I catch sight of the last trailing group member turning ahead. In my mind, I go over all the tips Christophe gave us, but quickly forget them as I worry about being left behind. I do a hockey stop at the turning point, stick my pole in and kind of jump round, my skis skidding beneath me. I manage to stay upright and slide off after my leader. I daren't look back for Barry, in case it tips me off balance. Then I hear him close behind, singing!

"Old MacDonald had a farm, EE-I-EE-I-O."

Parts of the slope are icy and my skis rattle as I skid across the top.

"Don't lose the leader," I mutter.

I'm not completely in control. I pick up speed, entirely by accident, fast approaching the girl in front. Sweating with fear, my fists grip the poles tightly. I feel my knees acting as shock absorbers below me as my skis clatter across the ice.

"Use the skis' edges!" I hear Christophe calling, though I can't see him. "Bend your knees, hips to the mountain."

I do as he instructs. I feel the skis lift on one side as my boots take the strain. The mist lifts away and I can see clearly again. From the side, the slope is so steep, it looks as if the world has been tilted, any further and I might fall off. Tiny snowballs tumble down the piste ahead of me, I can't keep up. The girl in front of me turns. Lurching forward I follow her lead and find my skis turning themselves as if they're on autopilot. I'm sure I didn't have much to do with it. Ahead, the line of skiers wriggles like an eel in Christophe's wake. My teeth are gritted together as I concentrate hard.

'Hips to the mountain, hips to the mountain,' I recite under my breath. We complete eight or nine turns and I don't really notice how far we travel. Christophe pulls up at the side of the piste, and gradually each skier takes the last bend and glides over to where the instructor waits. I glance at the group lining up beside Christophe. I need to tuck in at the bottom.

"There's Ralph. Ralph!" Hattie hollers, waving her ski poles in the air.

For a second I take my eyes off the girl in front, in order to look back up the mountain. An orange figure waits at the top. I spot Eve's green jacket in the Top Team making short, sharp turns down the side of the piste, like a bat flitting back and forth. She descends the black run so fast, like an expert. I'm mesmerized by her technique.

I lose concentration and hit a bump that unbalances me. My downhill ski flies up, but I manage to slap it back down and regain some control. When I look for the girl ahead, she's already made her turn and I didn't spot where.

"EE-I-EE-I-O. And on that farm they had some giraffes."

Giraffes! Now distracted by Barry's singing, I hit another bump hard. My knees bend trying to keep balance, but my skis are no longer on their edges. They fly up a hump until my bottom nearly hits the back of bindings.

"O-EE-O-EE-OOOO!" Barry scoots below me, narrowly missing the end of my ski pole. I try to push myself up but my skis have a mind of their own, sliding down the other side of the hump putting me completely off balance. I lean back and go even faster, my ski tips cross and I tumble dramatically several feet down the mountain, leaving my poles scattered up the piste behind me.

"Barney, Barney, Barney, what are we going to do with you?" sighs Christophe as he moves across to help.

I sit myself up, with nothing but my pride hurt. I hear the rhythmic sweeping noise of a skier fast approaching behind me until a sudden stop sprays me with snow. Imagine a falcon swooping down to pick up its prey. A gloved hand reaches over my shoulder holding my ski poles.

"Danke," Christophe is thanking the skier. He takes the poles for me and plants them in the snow. Then he rearranges my skis and pulls me up.

"Unlucky," says the skier still hovering behind me. I know exactly who it is, so I don't turn to face him. "At least you didn't split your pants."

"It's our first black run" belts Barry before I can stop him.

'I've done black runs before,' I want to shout.

I'm sure the skier laughs before he speeds off after his group.

***

I stab a piece of meat with my fondue fork and rest it inside the big pan of boiling oil. My plate's loaded with five pieces that I've already cooked, a jacket potato and corn on the cob smothered in butter. Mum offers me the salad bowl. I suppose I'd better get a few greens inside me too. I'm starving after all the skiing today.

"I only fell over once on the black runs," boasts Hattie.

"Well done," says Mum.

We went back to the north-face black run four times today. Once the cloud cleared, improving the visibility, it was much easier, but I still took a few more tumbles near the bottom. Trouble is, my legs get too tired and they just sort of give up. I now realise how strong the leg muscles of a proper skier must be.

"Olive didn't fall at all!" my sister continues. "She's a really good skier."

Mum's a good skier, much better than Olive. I quietly push the dangling tablecloth away and peer down at Mum's legs clad in skinny jeans. Her legs aren't big and muscly. Perhaps it's more to do with technique. I picture Eve, she tackled the run like it was easy. I wish I could be as good as her, then I'd be one of the best.

Anyhow, by the last run, I made a successful descent without a single fall. I think I've cracked the technique now. My skills only need a bit of polishing before I could take on anything.

I'm glad just my family and Barry are out at a restaurant on our own. I didn't want to be hanging around the hotel with all the others tonight. I know I fell over a lot and I don't need Ralph to remind me all evening. I hope Eve didn't see my wipeout. I bet Ralph told her though.

"I do like their outfits," says Mum admiring the waiters' and waitresses' traditional Austrian clothing. The ladies are in long dresses with puffy short sleeves. The men are wearing suede trousers that finish just below the knee with short collared-jackets to match.

"Grandpa would like it here," says Hattie pulling a chunk of bread dripping in cheese out of the other fondue. "I've seen pictures of him skiing in the old days when he wore long woolly socks pulled up to his knees over the top of his tweed trousers," she giggles.

"Did he?" Dad doesn't believe her.

"Yeah, there's a photo on his desk, haven't you seen it?" I ask Dad. He shakes his head. "He's wearing a bobble hat and a thick Aran jumper. Grandpa looks so funny with his climbing boots strapped to a pair of long, skinny, wooden skis."

"He even makes your own dad look modern," says Mum.

"What do you think of my new outfit then kids?" asks Dad stroking the sleeve of his new jacket, which is hanging on the back of his chair.

"A massive improvement," I say truthfully.

"Not too boring all in grey? Mum chose the darker colour for the salopettes. She says it makes me look taller." Dad raises his chin as he speaks, giving Mum a cheeky wink. Mum blows him a kiss. I cringe. It's embarrassing in front of my friend, but Barry doesn't even notice, too busy pushing more food onto his fondue fork.

"It's OK," Hattie shrugs, "not exactly cool. Black is cool for older men." Like Ralph's father she means.

"Black is boring," I spit. I rip a piece of meat off my fork. "Ow! That's hot!" I gulp down a glass of water.

"You've only just pulled it out of the pan Barney, what do you expect?" Mum kindly refills my glass of water.

"I like the go-faster stripes running down the side," pipes Barry. "I think they'll probably glow in the dark, along with that green flash on the back of your jacket. We'll easily be able to spot you on the blue runs."

"Yes, I do like to be conspicuous in the snow, especially on chair lifts," Dad laughs and so do Barry and I.

Hattie rolls her eyes. "I'm so glad I didn't have to witness that," she mutters beside me, so only I can hear.

At least Dad can take a joke. I bet Ralph's father can't. I wish Grandpa was here though.

CHAPTER 7

KEEPING SECRETS

As told by Barney

Dear Grandpa

It's been snowing all night. Cars are buried in snow. Mum says it'll be like skiing off piste since the snow is so deep.

Hattie and I can do black runs now without falling over (nearly). Dad's attempting a red run with his instructor today!

See you soon,

Barney

I chose a postcard of the mountain picturing our black run. So Grandpa can see where we skied, I mark the route with a big red arrow. I wonder if Grandpa ever did the same run when he was here many years ago, although I believe he said there were hardly any ski lifts when he visited, just a couple of long ropes to pull you up the hill. He said he'd hiked up carrying his skis. Sounds like hard work to me.

I head down to reception after breakfast to drop the card off for posting. I want it to arrive home before we do. As I reach the end of the corridor I spy Ralph coming out of the big posh suite. He's talking on the phone.

"I'll see you down there in just a minute. I'm leaving now, wait for me."

I nip around the corner and take the stairs far too quickly to avoid him seeing me. He's bound to rib me about my wipeout on the black run yesterday. I haven't seen him since then.

When I arrive at the boot room, Hattie is sat alone, already fastening her boots. She seems surprised to see me.

"What are you doing here?" she asks looking over my shoulder.

"Getting my boots like you," I reply, frowning. What an odd question.

"You're early, where's Barry? Shouldn't you be waiting for him?" she says, like she's telling me off.

"He'll be down soon," I shrug. "I've been to post a card to Grandpa."

Her eyebrows shoot up and her head does a little shiver.

"Are you alright Hattie?" I ask.

"Fine." She forces a grin.

I walk across to the shelves where all the boots are stacked. She thinks I'm not watching, but in one of the shop mirrors I catch her making hand signals to someone. I grab my boots and march back looking in the direction that she was signaling. A family with young kids making a lot of noise is walking through the shop. The little boy, who is already kitted up in his helmet and gloves, runs up to sit next to Hattie. She's distracted. More people arrive and soon the small place is full of children and adults putting on boots and pulling out skis. Eve arrives and sits beside me wedging her prosthetic into her ski boot, padding out the space with foam to stop the limb moving about. Thankfully she doesn't mention my black-run wipeout. Barry barges through the crowd. As he grabs his boots off the shelf, one of the undone clasps catches on another boot alongside it and he manages to pull several others down at the same time, all of them clattering to the ground. I walk over to help him clear up. When I return, Hattie's fully kitted out, holding her skis. Olive is sat booting up beside her and they're having a conversation, but Hattie's distracted, looking around as if she's waiting for someone else.

Mum and Dad appear out of the lift talking to the 'Secret Assassin'. Barry's right, he does look the business, but Dad's new outfit's not too bad either. I spot Ralph lurking in the background in the far corner of the shop, near where you get your skis waxed. Waxing them protects the underside of the skis and makes them go faster.

"Ralph's over there," I grumble to Barry. "I'll bet he'll want to play cards again tonight, so that he can beat us all and show off."

"He didn't win last time. Hattie won, twice," my friend reminds me.

"With Ralph's help," I point out.

"Why don't you ask him to help you next time?" he suggests.

"What!" It's bad enough that he's a better skier. I don't want him to think I can't play cards either. "Don't be ridiculous."

Suddenly I feel very hot in my helmet and jacket. I grab the rest of my gear. "I'll see you by the chair lift," I tell Barry as I pick up my skis and walk out into the blizzard.

I stomp through the thick snow. Everything seems to be happening in slow motion, people trudging along with their heads bent against the wind. I stop as close to the lifts as possible before dropping my skis onto the piste. One ski lands on the freshly pisted run whilst the other disappears into deep snow on the edge. I whack the bottom of my boots with my ski pole, trying to clear off clumps of snow stuck to the bottom. My left boot snaps easily into the ski binding. I lean across and drive my right boot into the ditch where my other ski lies. I stamp against the binding, but it just won't click around my boot. I lift my boot and try to clear more ice from the bottom as that might be stopping it. Again I try to fit my foot into the ski but it doesn't work. Leaning on my poles I puff out a big sigh. A small cloud billows from my mouth. I can hear Hattie and Olive chattering. Their voices getting louder as they approach.

"It'll be great fun," sings Hattie, "but I am a bit nervous."

"We can do it tomorrow after the races," Olive suggests. "You'll be fine."

"Yes of course, I know!" Hattie replies, slightly irritated.

"OK," says another voice.

A bunch of five year olds zoom over to the lift, along with their instructor. "Who do you..." I'm surrounded by screaming kids. "... win...?" I can't hear properly so don't recognise the voice. Maybe it's Eve? Nah, sounded a bit too gruff.

I concentrate on hitting my boot again, but it's difficult to see if there's any ice still stuck on the bottom.

"Barney! Wait for me," booms my big friend. I can always recognise his bellow.

I'm balancing on one leg, I'm not going anywhere quickly! Two small boys break out in a fight beside me, jumping about on their tiny skis and throwing snowballs at each other. One kid jumps my way knocking me flying into the soft snow. My goggles are coated in a fine spray and I get a mouthful of icy snowflakes.

Vijay, Hattie and Olive arrive in hysterics. They must have seen what just happened.

"Pull me up!" I poke Barry with a ski pole.

"It's the Abominable Barney," he jokes, dragging me out until I'm standing on one ski.

As Hattie shuffles past, I tap her on the arm.

"What were you talking about back there?" I ask as I bash the snow under my boot.

"Nothing." She shakes her head and moves on.

I try to snap my boot into the binding. My friends are moving away in the queue for the lift.

"I can't get my boot in. My ski binding is broken," I complain, stamping my foot against the ski. I'm going to get left behind.

Ralph suddenly appears beside me. He picks the offending ski out of the deep snow and hits the back of my binding with his fist until it snaps down.

"There you go Barney, you hadn't set it right, that's all." He brushes off any snow and places the ski down beside me.

Tentatively I push my boot tip into the front of the binding and snap my heel down at the back.

"Fixed!" He grins a big, wide toothy smile.

I peer into his visor but only see myself reflected back in its mirror.

"Thanks."

"I think Ralph will win," I hear my sister snigger to Olive from further up the queue.

"No problem." Ralph heads for the lift as if he hadn't heard the girls.

Why is Ralph good at everything? What is he going to win anyway?

CHAPTER 8

DEEP SNOW

As told by Barney

By the time we reach the top of the mountain, the blizzard has stopped. A faint glow in the sky tells me the sun is still alive. The sound of beeping piste bashers can be heard as they play catch up trying to clear the slopes. Christophe takes his Crazy Team to one side of a long, wide piste, to an area that hasn't been smoothed by the machines. Half a metre of fresh snow covers the ground. We line up in a rainbow of outfits. I'm beginning to realise that bright colours are good for being spotted on the mountain.

"We are going to travel through here." Our instructor flings one ski up into the air sprinkling us all with snowflakes.

"Hey!" laughs Vijay, as he takes the brunt of the shower.

"You need to keep your knees bent and close together as we bounce through the deep snow, keeping your body low," Christophe continues. "Remember keep your hips to the mountain. Don't lean back. Press your shins into the front of the boot."

Off-piste training, I've never done this before so I'd better concentrate if I've any chance of challenging Ralph to a race later in the week.

"Knees bent, shins on boots," Hattie mumbles, checking her position.

"I will go first to demonstrate. Wait for my signal, then you go one at a time, so I can watch you."

The girls are nodding.

Christophe glides through the snow, weaving a pathway. Back and forth he bounces like he's in a human pinball machine. Finally he stops some distance away, after making eight perfect, short turns like a giant paintbrush has swept a wiggly line through the surface . He waves his sticks in the air.

"Me first!" Vijay leaps forward, wearing his yellow-and-black-checkered helmet. This morning, he's extremely keen since his Dad bought him his very own striking helmet yesterday. "I want to be first to follow his tracks." He sets off in Christophe's exact, same line.

"I'm not sure you're supposed to do that," says Olive quietly.

We all watch. Tightly crouched, poles tucked under his bent arms, Vijay's small body slides through the first, second and third of Christophe's turns without a problem, but he doesn't seem to be bouncing in quite the same way as our instructor. His position is more like a statue leaning one way and then the other on each turn.

"Don't stay in my tracks!" Christophe shouts.

"I don't think Vijay heard that," says Hattie watching him race towards the fourth turn.

"He needs to make his own tracks," says Olive, "otherwise he'll keep going faster and faster." She seems to know a lot. I wonder if she's done this before.

Vijay jolts and jumps to make the fifth turn, his bent arms flapping like wings. Flying on to the sixth turn, still in Christophe's tracks, our friend is speeding up by the second.

"I don't think he's in control," I suggest to the rest of the group.

"Make your own tracks Vijay!" Christophe orders.

"Uh-oh too late!" Hattie whistles as Vijay misses the next turn, wobbling as he hits the deep snow. He automatically leans back, his little legs slicing through the powder without turning. In an instant his skis run away down under the surface, leaving his body trailing behind. The group takes a collective deep breath.

"Ooh!" gasp the girls.

Plop! Our friend falls into the snow, sending a great puff of snowflakes into the air. There's a hole in the surface where

Vijay was last seen. The yellow and black chequers of his helmet peep out like a warning sign.

Christophe side steps up to the place where Vijay disappeared. Peering down into the hollow he says, "are you OK my friend?"

A fluffy white body rises from the hole. "I'm the Abdominal Snowman!" Vijay cries out. He's such a funny little fella, making Christophe howl with laughter. "Small problem. I've lost a ski somewhere under all this snow." He flings his arms up into the air shaking off the snow.

Christophe is still laughing. "What am I going to do with you?"

They spend a few minutes poking about until they retrieve Vijay's ski.

"Well Vijay's obviously not going to win," Olive comments to Hattie.

Win what? I'm about to ask when Barry booms in my ear. "Abdominal Snowman, did you hear him?" He nudges me so hard I nearly fall over.

Christophe gets Vijay to do one big sweeping turn, then he waves for the next contestant.

"Olive, you go, show us what to do." Hattie gently pushes her friend forward.

Beaming, Olive takes a line parallel to Christophe's. Her skis cut through the snow with ease, creating a wake of ice dust, as she leaves a trail perfectly matching our instructor's.

"That's obviously what you're supposed to do," I remark.

"Bravo Olive!" Christophe congratulates her before waving his sticks in the air again.

"I don't think it's as easy as it looks," Hattie comments. "Wish me luck!"

My sister takes a line the other side of Christophe's tracks. You can tell she's nervous by the way she hunches over, gripping tightly on her poles. Her arms are like oak tree branches set in one position, whereas Olive's arms were like a willow tree's branches, effortlessly floating in the wind. Hattie does well for the first few turns, then she misses a turn, cutting across both Christophe's and Olive's tracks.

"Weight on the downhill ski!" Christophe reminds her, and she immediately changes her position, regaining control and finishing with a few more turns.

"Can't be that difficult if Hattie's done it. I reckon we'll be alright," I confide in Barry as we watch the other members of our group plunge into the deep snow.

"I'm not sure," says Barry, rubbing his chin with his glove. "I'm a lot heavier than Hattie. What if I sink into the snow?"

"You've got to keep the momentum going, that's the bouncing bit isn't it?" I tell him, even though I not too sure myself.

If we crack this, then off piste will be no problem. That'd show Ralph I can tackle anything on skis.

"If I bounce up and down, I reckon I'll look like I'm getting up and down off the loo over and over again." Barry curls his lip up to his nostril. I smirk. I should reassure him that's not true, but I don't.

"What do you think Olive's going on about winning? Is it the cards?" I change the subject. I'm determined to beat Ralph this evening. He's becoming too much of a show off. And he was rude about my dad and his unfortunate pant-splitting accident.

"Nah, I think it's about the race."

"Race, what race?" I ask.

"The ski groups all do a race towards the end of the week."

"Oh, hey do you reckon we could win?" My eyes light up. "That'd show Ralph, if me and you came back with medals."

"I'm up," cries Barry focusing on his skiing. "See you at the bottom." He tucks down and slides away, quickly picking up speed as he gets stuck in a set of tracks already made.

"Make your own tracks!" I call after him before he's too far away.

A quick flick of a stick tells me he heard. He leans sideways and diverts off at an angle. I get the giggles watching him overdo the bouncing. All I can think of is a big loo with a long pulley chain and Barry sitting down on it, farting and being propelled up again.

He doesn't do much turning, just one long diagonal line of bouncing. Ploughing through the snow like a big ship surging through the sea, he eventually stops at a point level with the group but about 20 metres to the left, so he has to pole over to them. Christophe appears to be having a quiet word and I was too busy giggling at the sight of Barry to notice Christophe's signal for me to start, but I push off anyway.

Most of the first section is almost like a piste now, where our group's skis have packed the snow down. I veer over to the far side to get into fresh powder. The initial tug on my skis as I hit the deep snow reminds me to bend my knees even more. I try my best to lean forward, frightened of speeding up out of control if I sit back. All I can think of is sitting on the toilet. I start chuckling as I try to stand up to make my next turn. I rise too far back, feeling my skis fly ahead. Immediately I crouch back down.

"Shins touch your boot Barney! Lean on the downhill ski!" I hear Christophe shouting instructions.

I slam my knees down and lean forward to squash my shins into my boots. It feels unnatural to be leaning so far down the mountain but I appear to have more control. I cruise through a couple of turns. I think I've got it. There'll be no beating me in the race, even in deep snow. Hang on, I'm off course. I'm too far left of the group, just like Barry. Drastic action is required and I decide to make a sweeping turn, leaning too hard on my downhill ski and promptly topple over right in front of the group and get a mouthful of cold snow.

I'm greeted with a round of applause, and Barry throws a snowball at me.

"You were doing so well until you lent over too far," explains Christophe. He offers out his pole, I grab it and he pulls me up. "It's all about the balance."

Easy for him to say. I stand tight lipped with my fists on my hips.

"Come on Crazy Team, we try again."

This does not bode well for any race against Ralph. Errors like this will be costly.

CHAPTER 9

BLIZZARD

As told by Barney

Up and down our chair swings and bounces in the wind as the lift halts. Suspended in mid air, we dangle above a deep crevasse. The snow blinds us. Sometimes we hear the muffled voices of skiers somewhere below us, shadowy figures in the distance. In the whiteout, snowflakes whip across in front of us, swirling like twisters. Our seat rocks back and forth. The chair ahead of us is empty and I can't see the chair behind. The visibility is deteriorating. I tug my scarf up to cover my nose to stop it freezing. Are we alone up here?

"Not again," moans Barry. "What happened to the view?" He reaches up and pulls the chair's plastic cover down, like a massive visor across the three of us. Immediately snow starts to stick to the surface, building up a small snowdrift along the rim.

"Must be your giant snowman shaking out his dandruff," I joke.

"Ha!" replies Barry, it wasn't really a laugh.

"Perhaps it's too windy," Vijay suggests, his teeth chattering.

"Well I hope they don't leave us here until the wind stops, otherwise we could be out all night." I bash my gloved hand against the plastic, trying to remove the collecting snow but it won't budge. It feels like we're being snowed in.

"Do you think they'll have to use a ladder to get us down?" Barry asks. I can tell by his unusually squeaky voice, he thinks that'd be exciting.

I look down past my skis at the jagged rock face below us, like an open mouth of sharp teeth waiting for dinner.

"We're above a crevasse. How are they going to get a ladder up from that?"

"They'll just wait for a lull in the wind and we'll move on, I'm sure." Vijay knows everything.

"So how far is this race?" I wonder out loud, trying to take my mind off the crevasse and the eyes on my skis.

"They're marking the course out tomorrow morning. It'll start at the hut part way down Blue run number 4," says Vijay. I told you he knows everything.

"That's the one that goes down to our hotel isn't it?" Barry checks.

"Yes, I believe there are going to be 10 gates to ski around. We'll be able to have a few practice runs early morning with Christophe. Racing starts at 11 o'clock."

"How do you know all this Vijay?"

"I have spoken with our instructor, and my father consulted the programme of events on the hotel notice board last night."

"I didn't even know there was a notice board," I admit. "We need to work out how soon we should tuck down to get the best time, without missing any of the gates."

"I'm just gonna tuck from the top," declares Barry.

"I'd be amazed if you make it past gate number three if you do that!" Vijay warns him.

The chair jars and the lift tarts moving momentarily before jolting to a halt once again.

My fellow passengers go quiet.

"It must be nearly four o'clock, it'll be getting dark soon," I sigh.

"Yeah, and you know what comes out at dusk," Barry warns. "Abdominal…"

"Abominable!" Vijay and I chorus together, correcting him.

"As I was saying…" Barry starts again and stops abruptly as the chair lifts judders.

The silence is broken by a thud, a loud crack and several faint squeals.

"Oh crickey!" Vijay's helmet sinks onto his shoulders. "The Abominable Snowman!"

My friends and I shuffle closer together without speaking. I wish I were sitting in the middle, like Barry, and not on the edge. The horrible snowman's bound to pick off the easiest catch first. Perhaps Vijay looks tastier than me. Then I feel guilty for hoping that to be the case. Maybe it's smell that attracts him. I dip my head trying to sniff my armpits. I wish I'd washed this morning.

The blizzard is swirling around us and I'm starting to feel dizzy. The three of us bunch together, shivering in silence. A high-pitch screech of mangled metal pierces the air.

"He's probably stepped on a piste basher!" whispers Barry.

"Flying footballs," murmurs Vijay.

"What if we've been forgotten?" I raise the question. I daren't look down in case I see a pair of eyes glowing out of the deep crevasse. I'm starting to panic. "I think we should call for help."

A strong, howling gust hits our chair, making it swing. There's no more discussion. We all instantly agree and cry out.

"HELP!"

The chair lift cranks into action and within seconds we are in sight of the top of the lift and the rest of our group. I'm so relieved. I let go a squeaky fart, it slips out by accident. At least it'll scare off the Abominable Snowman.

CHAPTER 10

CHEAT

As told by Barney

"Was it you lot crying for help?" Olive asks us that evening as we sit in the lounge with Ralph dealing out the cards.

Vijay's eyes nearly pop out as he's looking at me, like a rabbit in headlights. He's mouthing something to me, slowly shaking his head.

"Of course it was," laughs Hattie.

Olive retells the story of the blizzard on the chair lift. She and Hattie were two cars ahead of us, though we couldn't see them at the time. She's making it sound really scary until she mimics our cry for help. Ralph and Eve find it amusing.

"Scared you were trapped on the mountain with the Abominable Snowman?" Ralph cackles.

"No," I snap back, a bit too quickly. I don't want him to know that I was frightened. I inhale deeply through my nose and pretend to be calm. I can feel my cheeks burning up, so I divert their attention by pulling my jumper off over my head.

"No, it wasn't Barney," says Barry, very matter of fact. "It wasn't Vijay either."

Ralph stops dealing and looks up at Barry. I stare at him too, so does Vijay.

"It was me," he plainly states. "I thought we were stuck on the lift and been forgotten. It was getting darker, what with the blizzard, and I thought we needed to get home safe before the Abdom…"

"Abom…" Vijay quietly starts to correct him.

Barry nods and continues. "The horrible snowman came out. So I shouted for help."

"Sounded like more than one person shouting to me," Olive teases. There's a slither of nastiness in Olive that I haven't seen before and I don't like it. I think she's trying to show off to impress Ralph. I thought she liked me.

"It's the mountain, creates an echo," Vijay explains. He's so clever, Olive chooses not to argue with him.

"Can we start the game?" says Eve. She picks up her cards.

We're playing the game of cheat. The whole pack of cards is dealt out between the players. Eve begins by placing two cards, one on top of the other, onto to the table. The cards are facing down so we can't see what she's playing.

"Two 10s," she says.

That means Vijay must put down either 10s, jacks or 9s. If I had three 10s myself, then I'd know that Eve was cheating, otherwise I'd have to accept that she's telling the truth.

If you think someone's cheating, you call out "Cheat", then the cards are turned over to display what was actually played. If they did cheat, they pick up all the cards. If they didn't cheat, the accuser picks up the pile. The winner is the first to get rid of all their cards.

I fan out my cards only to see the Ace of Snowmen glaring back at me. I gulp.

"One nine," says Vijay. I don't reckon Vijay ever cheats. He's far too honest.

"Three, no… two eights, sorry," says Olive taking her turn.

Hmm, suspicious.

"Two sevens," Hattie quickly follows slapping her hand down.

Ralph selects his cards carefully. He turns his head to look first at Olive, and then at Hattie sat beside him. Is he trying to look at Hattie's hand? He chews on his lips before pulling his cards out and placing them onto the pile.

"Two eights," he announces, glaring at Olive as he does so.

But he can't have two eights, because I've got two eights and Olive's already put two eights on to the pile. There are only four eights in the whole pack.

Barry's selecting cards from his hand.

"Cheat!" I yelp, pointing at Ralph and preventing Barry from playing his card.

Ralph's eyebrows twitch, his mocking smile immediately tells me I'm wrong. He turns over the last two cards on top of the pile, the eight of clubs and the eight of diamonds.

"It wasn't me who cheated," he raises his eyebrows at the girls.

I frown, collecting up the rest of the pile. Olive bows her head sheepishly. I survey the cards to see that she put down a three and a five. She cheated and got away with it. Seems I misjudged Ralph.

Vijay wins three out of four games. I can't help thinking how lucky he must be with all the cards he is dealt. I think I'm too quick to react in this game. I seem to collect up more cards that I ever manage to put down.

Ralph is packing away the cards. "Are you all doing the race tomorrow?" he asks.

"Definitely," Hattie is the first to reply. "I'm going to be super speedy." She tucks down, leaning right then left as if she's negotiating the ski poles in the race. "Any tips?" she asks Ralph.

He straightens up as he puts the pack in his pocket. "Be sure to make all the gates," he advises her.

"I am going to count them on our practice runs, then I'll know what I've got to do in the real race." Everything is mathematical with Vijay.

"I'm just gonna tuck from the top. Christophe says that heavy people go fast that's why he's always at the front," Barry announces.

"He goes at the front because he's the instructor," I point out. Barry eyes me suspiciously. Then I feel bad, what if I've embarrassed him after he stuck up for Vijay and me earlier, so I add "but you might be right."

The corners of Barry's mouth turn up exposing his two front teeth.

"Maybe you won't get beaten by my little brother then Barney!" Ralph jokes. "Good luck."

I bite my top lip. Hattie and Olive snigger. Ralph glances at the girls. He's got some new admirers and he loves it.

"I think you'll win tomorrow Ralph," I hear Hattie twitter to him as we all get up to leave.

"Me too," Olive butts in. The girls are both fluttering their eyelashes. Yuk! I think I may puke.

Eve rolls her eyes. "Goodnight, see you all at the races."

"Night Eve," Barry's booming voice stands out against the crowd.

Barry and I walk away and as soon as we're out of earshot, I say "If we do anything tomorrow, we have to win that race."

CHAPTER 11

SKI RACE

As told by Barney

"We're meeting him at lunch and skiing together this afternoon," Olive tells Hattie as the Crazy Team waits for the race to begin.

There's a light wind and bright sunshine, perfect conditions for racing. The slopes have been groomed, so no deep snow.

"Skiing with who?" I interrupt their conversation.

"Ralph," says Olive. "Are you coming?"

Lessons finish at the end of this morning, so we can ski with our families after lunch.

"Aren't we skiing with Mum and Dad?" I say to Hattie.

"Dad's not going to be able to ski very far is he?" she snorts.

I feel like she's mocking him. He might not be very good, but at least he's trying. I thought it'd be fun to do a bit of skiing with them both. Mum usually buys us a great big hot chocolate whenever we ski together. In a mountain restaurant I noticed someone having this chocolate drink piled high with whipped cream, marshmallows and chocolate flakes. Looks fab. I'm hoping to direct Mum there this afternoon.

"My parents only ski for an hour after lunch," Olive informs me. "Ralph's dad's got a conference call to take and his mum's got a massage booked at two, so Ralph's free straight after lunch."

"I'm sure they won't want to ski with us all afternoon," Hattie back tracks. "How about we ski with them for an hour and then meet our friends?" she pleads with me. "Please Barney, it'll be fun, like an adventure."

"I don't think they'll let us just ski off!" I scoff. We've never skied on our own before.

"Why don't you agree on an area that you're allowed to stick to? That's what I've done with my parents when I was skiing with my older cousins." Olive has it all planned out, so it's difficult for Hattie to say no.

"Wish me luck guys!" Vijay yelps as he quickly poles away from the gate, racing against Oscar. His undone jacket flaps against his sides like wings, he may take off at any minute. "One…two…" I hear him counting as he navigates his way through the gates at a steady pace. Oscar already takes a metre lead before they both drop away and disappear over the hill.

"Go on Vijay!" blasts Barry as the yellow-and-black-chequered helmet vanishes.

I'm pretty confident that I can beat Vijay.

Hattie moves up to the start line. She looks back at the stack of groups waiting to race. An orange figure standing near the back of the groups waves his pole at her.

"What's going on with your sister and Ralph?" queries Barry, having noticed the communication too.

"I've no idea." I shake my head.

Olive lines up at the start to race against her friend and focuses on the starter flag. It goes down and the two girls push off. Hattie is poling, whilst Olive chooses to skate her skis away from the start. Both girls reach the first gate together. Almost synchronised they glide around each pole, Hattie crunched into her tuck position, whilst Olive's more curled over. They disappear over the hill together, barely a millisecond between them.

Barry and I head down to the start.

"The loser has to bring the other one breakfast in bed!" he calls out.

"No, the loser has to carry the other one's skis back to the boot room. I hate that trudge across the snow."

Barry digs himself into position and licks his lips. "I'll have a waffle with berries and chocolate sauce please."

"What makes you think you're going to win?"

"I'm heavier remember." He crouches down.

The flag drops and we're off.

My arms move fast, digging my poles into the snow again and again to give me the best start. As I take the first turn, I peek over towards Barry. We're dead level. I crouch further forward and nearly go off balance but manage to stay with Barry up until the brow of the hill. The slow slope gives away sharply and my friend edges ahead. Not looking where I'm going, I hit a few ruts in the piste and bump about. I have to widen my skis to avoid a hole in the piste where someone must've fallen. I lose speed and Barry increases his lead. I need to turn tight to make the next gate. I curse myself for not concentrating on my own race, clipping the pole against my glove.

A red blob is at the top corner of my vision as I prepare for the last two gates. Heading down to the cheering crowd I know I'm beaten, but providing I'm second I'll be happy. Clearing the final gate I tuck so low, I'm nearly sitting on my skis, flying across the line. I rise up and perform an expert hockey stop.

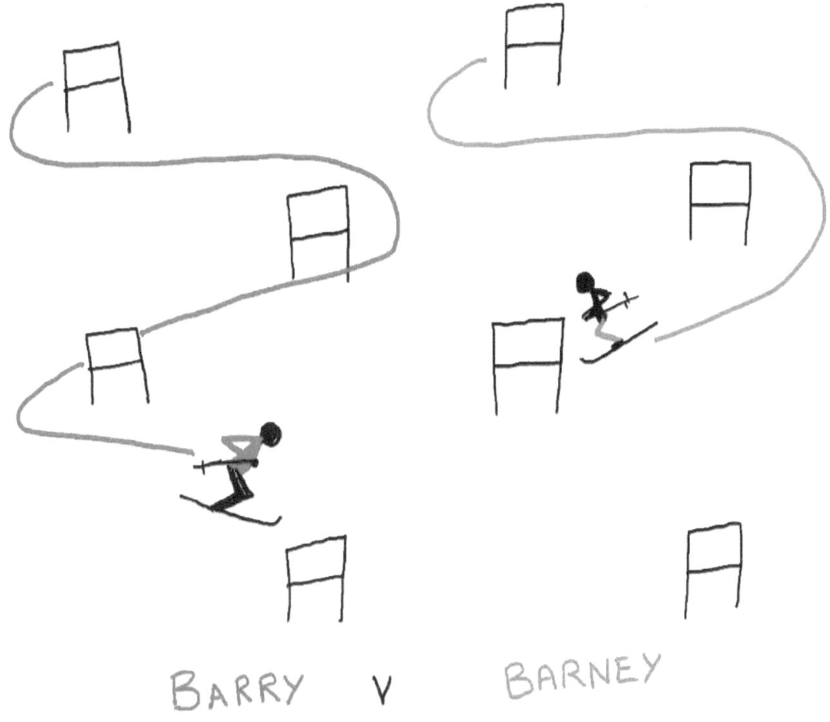

"Looks like I'm on breakfast duty." I reach out to fist pump Barry.

"Barney! Well done, you're in first ahead of Olive," claps Christophe walking across to the two of us. I turn to look back at the time.

"What about Barry?" I query, "he beat me across the line by a couple of metres."

"Yes, he was very fast, but we must wait to see how many penalties he has to add."

"I was going so fast I missed a gate, maybe two…, or three. I was like a rocket!" Barry amazes me, even if he doesn't win he's still happy.

"If he gets one penalty then he's in joint lead, but if he gets two penalties then he's not." Vijay has done all the necessary calculations.

"How did you do?" I feel it's only fair to ask.

"I'm down in one piece didn't fall over, unlike Oscar, who nearly took out half of the crowd."

"Barney!" I hear someone calling out my name.

"Mum." I spy her in the crowd waving.

She holds out her phone. "I've got it all on camera!" she calls out. "I've even worked out how to video."

"Where's Dad?" I bellow back.

"He'll be here soon."

At least I think that's what she said. It's difficult to hear as the next pair of skiers arrive. Shame, I wanted Dad to watch my race. I wonder where his ski group has been this morning.

Bright sunshine bounces off the snow. As racing continues the lower section becomes slushy, slowing the skiers down, which acts as an advantage to those who skied the track earlier. We watch many more skiers compete down the course until it's finally Eve versus Ralph. Remarkably I'm still in the lead.

"Did you know they were going to be paired against each other?" I ask Hattie as we watch the pair zigzag through the course. They both stick close to the fastest line, clipping the gates as they fly past.

"Ralph told me they probably would, as Eve's one of the best in their group. Come on Ralph!" Hattie cries out as the green and orange skiers both fly a jump over the hill. They soar through the air, knees tucked up.

"Go Eve!" I yell. If I'm going to be beaten by someone, I'd rather it was Eve. She's amazing and she never shows off like Ralph does.

The time is really fast, the seconds ticking by. My stomach churns as they eat away at my lead. Barely moving off course, they take the straightest line through the gates. Ralph's taking the race so seriously, wearing racing guards on his knees and arms to hit off the poles. Inseparable, they duck across the finish line. I swivel to look at the time. Three seconds faster than me. I'm well beaten.

"Yeah!" Hattie and Olive are jumping up and down cheering.

Ralph waves like a superstar to his fans.

"He didn't win," I point out to the girls. "He drew with Eve."

They ignore me. Hattie is trying to take a selfie, with Ralph in the background.

"There is one last skier," the announcement comes across the speakers at the bottom of the slope.

The crowd hushes and everyone looks up the mountain. A large grey figure stands poised to push off. It's tricky to see as the sun is blinding.

"They call him Lightning Flash!"

Vijay races over wide-eyed and wide-mouthed too. "It's your dad!" he tugs at my sleeve. "Lightning Flash, he's using the name I gave him."

I feel all colour drain from my face.

"Dad!" cries Hattie in horror, flinging her hands up and clawing at her cheeks. "This is so embarrassing."

Ralph is laughing with his Top Team mates. "If it was my dad, then I might be worried about my time, but not Barney's dad," I hear him say.

"Don't be so sure," Eve warns him. At least someone's sticking up for Dad.

"Race like the wind, Lightning Flash," yelps Mum.

"Mum!" Hattie growls glaring at her.

"Let's hope he doesn't split his pants again!" I hear Ralph joke.

He thinks my dad's rubbish.

The flag goes down and Dad's figure bobs along pushing out of the gates.

"Is he doing snow plough?" someone jokes.

I feel my chin sinking into my jacket. Please don't humiliate me Dad. I can barely watch.

"Lightning Flash! Lightning Flash!" Barry starts to cheer.

"What are you doing?" I talk through gritted teeth.

"Lightning Flash, Lightning Flash!" Vijay chants.

Eve joins in whilst the rest of the Top Team keep quiet, all precious about their times. Are they really worried?

Chanting builds through the crowd but Hattie and Olive remain mute too. I look up to see Dad suddenly flying through the air, his skis parallel but wide apart, his silhouette blocking out the sun. He smashes down with an unsteady landing, thundering past the next gate. Wow!

"Go Dad!" I push to the front, waving my fist in the air. I'm not sure how much control he's got zooming down the race course. "Come on Dad!" I yell.

Racing through gates seven and eight in a kind of parallel snowplough, his pace is ferocious. Clipping nine, he's off balance. One ski flies up in the air as he clatters past gate ten on one leg. Will he fall at the final hurdle? I hold my breath willing his ski to reconnect with the piste. Storming over the finish line, he's clear!

The crowd parts as he skates past, desperately trying to stop in the slush. Boom! He crashes into a big pile of soft snow, creating a deep crater. Soggy lumps of wet snow fly up everywhere like a volcano erupting.

I chase after him.

"Dad! Dad!"

"Barney, is that you?"

He sits up, his face and helmet covered in snow. I wipe it away from his goggles and look deep into his eyes, holding his head in my hands.

"You were the best Dad!"

"Lightning Flash!" Vijay cheers as he runs up beside me.

"You won Mr Frank!" Barry claps.

"Was I that good son?" Dad asks me, his cheeks dripping in melting snowflakes.

"Dad, you were Franktastic!"

I hug him with all my might.

CHAPTER 12

LIGHTNING FLASH

As told by Barney

A red-and-white striped ribbon hangs around Dad's neck. The
gold medal twinkles in the restaurant lights. Hattie's barely
spoken all lunch. Instead she's sitting slumped in the
cushioned wooden pew, slurping her soup. I've noticed she's

on the phone under the table, probably busy arranging her secret skiing plans for this afternoon. Straight after losing the race to Dad, Ralph ignored her, but they've made friends again.

Apparently Dad's skiing embarrasses her in front of all her friends. She still hasn't forgiven him, not that she's even explained it to Dad. Instead she mopes about trying to ignore the rest of the family.

"I didn't realise there was such a drop off the mountain part way down the course. We'd only skied the course once, slowly, first thing this morning." Dad is talking us through the race, gate by gate for the third time. He puffs out his chest showing off his gold medal. "I knew I was fast and when I heard you all cheering, that spurred me on."

"I started the cheering," beams Barry. "Lightning Flash, Lightning Flash!"

Hattie jumps, her body stiffening, and she glares at Barry. If she could fire lasers from her eyes, he would be in real trouble right now.

His chanting fades and Dad continues. "I knew I had to make all the gates. My leg muscles were burning but I drove through the pain. When I clipped a gate that flung me off balance, it nearly finished me off."

"I thought you were toast!" admits Barry.

"I didn't," I butt in. "I knew you could do it Dad."

Dad sits up straight and takes hold of his gold medal in one hand. He gulps a few times and is about to say something when the waitress arrives.

"From the gentleman in the black polo neck jumper," she explains, nodding towards Ralph's family. The waitress places two glasses of bubbling Champagne in front of Mum and Dad.

"Oh well, thank you. Danke," Dad says to the waitress. He quickly wipes his watery left eye with the napkin.

Hattie suddenly wakes up, puts down her spoon and stretches her neck to look across the restaurant.

"Congratulations on the gold medal," Ralph's father calls over.

"How thoughtful," says Mum, taking a quick sip of Champagne. "Such a charming man."

Dad raises his glass in the air and nods towards Ralph's father. Their whole family is looking our way.

"Thank you. Cheers!" Dad replies. "Or should I say 'bottoms-up'?" he chuckles quietly to our table.

"No Dad, not after the suit ripping incident," I urge.

Ralph's mum raises her diamond-ringed fingers and performs a little clap. Even Ralph picks up his sparkling water and toasts my dad. I notice that he's not wearing his silver medal.

"Yeah well done Dad," Hattie finally makes an effort, doing the same with her glass of juice.

"Lightning Flash!" toasts Barry, at which Hattie still winces.

"Lightning Flash!" Mum and I join the celebration.

***

Dad's face is as red as a beetroot. He forgot to put on any sun protection this morning and is already feeling the effect of the mountain sun. His legs muscles are seizing up too.

"Ow!" He grabs onto Mum's arm as he tries to get up from the lunch table. "I just need a bit of help dear."

Mum bends at the knee under the strain of helping to lift Dad off the chair. Taking a lot of weight, she is holding him under his armpits, which probably stink after a morning of skiing. He's always so sweaty with big wet patches on his thermals.

"Ye-ow!" He sounds like a cat meowing.

"Are you in pain?" Mum asks.

"Of course I'm in pain!" he snaps back. Dad never deals well with pain. I always remember the time he hopped around the kitchen yelping when he got a paper-cut opening an envelope.

"Perhaps we should take the cable car back down the mountain," suggests Mum. "Probably best you soak in a hot bath."

"Yes, I think that is a very good idea." Dad begins to calm down and flops back into his seat.

"What about us?" I stick out my bottom lip. "Can't we ski this afternoon either?" My shoulders sink and my smile sags.

"We can ski with our friends!" Hattie pipes, seizing her chance.

"Well I…" Mum hesitates.

I screw up my nose. I really wanted one of those hot chocolates and I know exactly where they sell them. We'll never get one unless Mum's with us.

"Olive's parents let her ski on her own on certain slopes," Hattie begins scheming.

That's not strictly true. I'm sure she was with her older cousins at the time.

"And Ralph is going to ski alone this afternoon, so we could ski with him and he's a really good skier." Her eyes open wide as she glances at our parents. She sidles up next to Dad and rests her head against his arm. "He's not as good as you though, Lightning Flash." It's sickly stuff.

Mum and Dad are looking at each other considering the options. Just at that moment Ralph's mother reappears in the restaurant. Their family had left 10 minutes ago. She walks up to the table where they were sitting and retrieves her gold helmet. Mum follows my gaze and spots Ralph's mother.

"I'll just ask Ralph's mother what she thinks," says Mum. She begins to walk away from our table over to where Ralph's mother is tucking her curly hair into the shiny helmet.

Hattie's hands clench the table, nearly pulling the tablecloth off. We all watch Mum in conversation with the gold helmet. All except Dad, who's too busy rubbing his sore legs. Huge diamond rocks twinkle in the restaurant lights as Ralph's mother animates their discussion.

Mum returns as the gold helmet leaves the restaurant.

"What did she say?" Hattie jumps to ask.

"She thinks it'll be fine. She's going back to the hotel. Ralph's little brother is having a private lesson with Christophe apparently. They're going to be on Blue 4, which takes you back to the hotel. So Ralph has been told to stick to Blue 4 and Red 7. The two chair lifts meet at the top. Any problems and Ralph has Christophe's number."

"All sorted then," Hattie stands up, picking up her gloves and helmet.

"Um…" Dad seems unsure. "What about his father?"

"He's gone to the hotel for a conference call, but then he'll come back out onto those slopes to find Ralph after that," Mum explains.

I sense Dad's reluctance to agree with the arrangements. "Who else is going to be with you?"

Hattie's phone pings. She slides her finger across the screen. "Oh, it's Ralph," she twitters. "I guess his mum must have told him. He's waiting outside. And Olive's there too."

"Perhaps Olive's dad could ski with you all?" suggests Dad. "I'm sure he'd be understanding about my predicament. I think I injured myself on that last gate."

"No!" Hattie quickly snaps. "No, I err...mean, no they want Olive to err...start learning..." she's making this up I can tell, "...to be independent. Like when she gets the bus to school."

Dad's eyebrows nearly meet in the middle as he frowns. "What's skiing got to do with getting the bus?"

Hattie draws breath, her mouth open wide. I know that her brain is working hard to try and figure this one out. She's telling fibs, I'm sure of it. But I want to stay out skiing, so I keep quiet.

"Hattie, there you are, Olive's looking for you, she's waiting to go skiing." We all turn, as Olive's dad walks into the restaurant. "Oh dear mate, what happened to your face? Bit of sun burn there!" He directs his comments at Dad, whose face is so burning hot you could toast marshmallows on it.

"So are you skiing with the kids?" Dad asks him hopefully.

"No, I've agreed to stay in this restaurant, help myself to one of those delicious desserts and maybe a cheeky glass of something. Why don't you both join me, the missus will be back in a minute too. Olive knows where we are if there's a problem, and they promise to stay on runs 4 and 7. We'll rendezvous at 3.30pm to ski down together."

"Oh, well," Dad relaxes back into his chair, peeling his jacket off his shoulders. "I suppose we could wait around for a while couldn't we dear?" Dad looks up at Mum. It seems that his return to the hotel isn't so urgent after all.

"Promise to be careful kids," Mum waggles her forefinger at the three of us. "No showing off and racing, otherwise you'll end up croc like your father."

"Promise Mum," Hattie skips by. "You were terrific today Dad, Lightning Flash." She kisses Dad on the forehead. His bright red cheeks bulge as he smiles. "Let's go!" Hattie hisses the order at Barry and me, tilting her head towards the door.

"Don't be late back either," Mum warns.

I hesitate. Leaning across to Mum I whisper "Can we have one of those hot chocolates when we get back?"

"As long as you are back on time," says Mum, tapping her watch, "and no racing."

I fake a faint smile and make no promises.

CHAPTER 13

A TEAM SPLIT

As told by Barney

Ralph is racing ahead but I manage to keep up. Blue 4 is a long run, all the way down the valley past our hotel. The top section can be icy in the mornings, but this afternoon following a morning of bright sunshine this section is just right to ski on. The surface has a thin soft layer above the compact ice.

I try to mimic Ralph's actions; he's as good as an instructor to follow, even if I do hate to admit it. If he bends his knees lower, then I do the same. When he straightens up on a turn, I lengthen my legs too. I even copy his pole plants.

My legs are a bit wobbly when we stop part way down for a rest. I've been concentrating on digging the edges of my skis into the piste.

"I love that long run," says Ralph as we wait for everyone else to arrive.

"Yes, it's quite easy to zigzag across the slope, no big humps," I agree.

"Yeah, you can go super fast too, providing there isn't anybody else in your way." Ralph points up the mountain to where Hattie and Olive are negotiating their way through a group of small kids. "That's why I stuck to the left-hand side because of that group on the right. The girls should've followed my lead."

"Flying footballs!" yelps Barry as he bounces over the only bump on the piste and crash lands at my feet.

"Are you ever in control Barry?" laughs Ralph.

My big friend ignores Ralph's remark. "Give us a hand up Barney."

We wait for the girls.

"This is where you come out if you cut across off piste from Red 7." Ralph uses his pole to point out a series of tracks in the deep snow linking up to the piste. Someone's stuck a yellow bobble hat on the top of the blue stake that marks the edge of piste. "There are several routes you can take."

"Have you done it then?" Barry asks.

"Yeah, of course I have." He gives his shoulders a shuffle. "Our group did it with our instructor yesterday, and I've done it several times before with my father."

"Is that why you wear that rucksack? Has it got off-piste stuff in there?" I'd heard Olive talking about Ralph's rucksack, but I didn't really know what was in there.

"Yeah, it's got a set of elongating poles to poke down into the snow to find someone buried beneath, and a shovel to dig them out," Ralph explains.

"If there's an avalanche you mean?"

Ralph answers Barry's question with a nod.

"How would you know where to find them?" Surely you couldn't just go poking about in the snow hoping that you'd come across them? It'd be like finding a needle in a haystack (that's one of Grandpa's sayings).

"I'm wearing a transceiver that sends out signals." He pulls up the bottom of his jacket to show the grey box that he wears tucked along the top of his salopettes. I had noticed it before. It has straps that go around his waist and diagonally across his body up over one shoulder. "You must have this on. You turn the dial to detect, and then it picks up any other signals close by. So when you get near another transceiver, the beeps start getting much closer together. So you can mark out a small area using gloves or anything you've got on you, to show where the signal is strongest. That's where you start plunging your pole in until you hit something squashy like a person rather than something hard like a rock."

The girls arrive.

"Sorry, we got caught up," puffs Hattie, a little out of breath.

"I had to help a little boy who'd fallen over and lost his skis," says Olive.

Ralph pulls his jacket over the transceiver. "Are you ready to get onto the chair lift?"

"Yes!" cries Hattie, already angling her skis down the slope. "You can follow us." She slides away.

The two girls and Ralph reach the chair lift first, but Ralph breaks away from chatting to the girls, choosing to hold back and get on the lift with Barry and me. On the way up he tells us about all the off piste runs he's done with his father, and ones that he'd like to do when he's older, dropping into fresh powder snow where no one else has been. They'd go out in the mornings and disappear off the rugged back of a mountain.

"Skiing in remote valleys is incredible," Ralph raves. I'm gripped. "One time, we were all alone when a mountain goat trotted down a cliff face ahead of us."

"I think I saw a mountain goat from this chair lift yesterday," claims Barry, jumping in. He never mentioned it before.

"And an eagle circled overhead," Ralph continues.

"Cool," I murmur. Their adventures sound so exciting.

"My father used to be in the army and trained people to ski."

"I told you," Barry whispers in my ear as Ralph divulges this information. "A real secret assassin," he whispers. Luckily, I don't think Ralph hears.

I'm dying to ask whether he was in the Special Forces doing secret undercover operations. He certainly looks like he could've been by the way he dresses on the slopes, like a James Bond character. Come to think of it, he does suddenly appear out of nowhere, like when he returned Barry's ski, and he quickly disappears too. Although I wonder if he should be in some sort of white camouflage gear, rather than black.

"The mountains can be very dangerous places," Ralph warns. "My father always checks out the snow before he lets me ski down, so as not to cause an avalanche. He tells me that if you do get caught, you should try to cup your hands to your face so that you've got a little air pocket if you get buried." Ralph demonstrates. "Once you've stopped falling, if you dribble spit you'll be able to see which way is up and which way is down." He leans out over the hand bar of the chair and dribbles out a line of spit. It dangles away from his face until it drops onto the snow, catching on a branch of a fir tree. "Gravity will pull your spit down." Ralph's dad sounds like a survival guru.

My mouth is open in awe, while Barry's mouth is testing out the dribble theory.

"This is the route," says Ralph, shuffling to the edge of the chair, tapping excitedly on my shoulder. "Look, can you see those tracks Barney, up above that old mountain hut?" He points to a clump of fir trees, hiding an old shack. Several skiers' tracks are carved into the deep snow. With the sun out, you can spot them easily as the crystals twinkle in the fresh snow and not in the contours of the tracks. I can see them now, but as the sun disappears behind the clouds, the light dulls and they are harder to pick out.

"Those are the tracks you follow from Red 7," he claims.

I notice a patch just across from there that appears riddled with rocks. You'd want to steer clear of that for sure. I look further up the mountain but I can't see where the tracks come out over the hill, as there are row upon row of grand fir trees in the way, their arms dripping in snow like white icing. I can only see the very top of the mountain in the distance, up where the two chair lifts meet. Red 7 is much steeper at the top and drops down the other side of the mountain.

"Look, isn't that your little brother with Christophe?" Barry signals to a small child following an instructor on the blue run. Ski-school instructors are easy to spot because they all wear the same gear, so the whole team match. Ralph's brother is easy spot, too. Dressed head to toe in bright green, he looks like a big frog bouncing about the slopes. "Christophe!" Barry starts waving, but they pass below us and obviously can't hear him. "Aw."

"Your brother's a really good skier," I say.

"It's easy when you're six because you don't have far to fall. He doesn't really have to bend his legs much as he's so tiny, so my mother says. My father thinks he'll be a better skier than me." Ralph hangs out of the side of the chair, watching his brother ski by. His bottom lip droops and he looks a bit sad.

"How old were you when you first learnt to ski?" I ask him.

"Four. You?"

"Eight." It sounds so old compared with Ralph, so I add. "But I've been three times now."

"I've only ever been twice," Barry states. "Once on a school trip when I was 10, coz my mum doesn't ski. We can't really afford it. The other time my uncle paid for all the family to go for a weekend to celebrate his birthday."

"What did your mum do then?" I ask.

"A lot of window shopping," he replies.

"We ski twice a year," adds Ralph, which trumps my three trips in a lifetime. "So I'm kind of expected to be good."

I don't think he's boasting, he's just stating the truth. I am jealous though. His father's a secret agent, he can ski down virtually anything and knows loads of cool survival stuff. My dad's sat in the café because his legs hurt after barely surviving a ski race against children. And he split his salopettes on this very chair lift. I sigh.

We don't really talk much for the rest of the ride up, each of us lost in our own thoughts.

"We'll follow you, shall we Ralph?" suggests Hattie smiling at Ralph as the five of us stand at the top of Red 7.

Olive is bent down refastening her ski-boot clips whilst Barry is wiping the fog off his goggles. My hands begin to shake. I'm always a bit nervous at the top of this one, as it's so steep. Another run cuts across it part way down, so you have to be careful not to crash into other skiers coming from different directions. It's the equivalent of Piccadilly Circus without any traffic lights. I know I can do it so why do I get nervous? Usually, I try and get right behind our instructor for this bit. Without Christophe, I was at least hoping to follow Ralph but it appears that Hattie's bagging that spot.

"Will you wait for me on this section Barney?" Barry tugs on my sleeve. "I'm not very good at avoiding other people on this bit."

"Err…" I hesitate. Barry tends to overtake me at critical moments. Like when I'm about to make a turn, he cuts in, meaning I have to go in the opposite direction to avoid a collision.

Ralph leans over and speaks to Hattie privately.

"Yeah, OK," I hear her say.

"Why don't I wait for you Barry? You can follow me if you like," Ralph offers. "The girls can go ahead and meet us further down."

"And I'll keep up the rear," I hastily add. At least I'll be close to Ralph and can watch where he turns.

"See you shortly." Olive waves her mittens at us.

"We'll take the right-hand route, where it's quieter, and meet you just past the bend," Hattie informs us of her plans. The run splits a few hundred metres away, linking back together further down the piste. One side is a little steeper, which is not ideal, but it tends to be quieter so there's less chance of a collision.

"That's the place," Ralph nods. Have they already agreed some plan of action here? "Right Barry, follow me. I'll take it steady to avoid the traffic."

The girls disappear quickly whilst Ralph slowly curls back and forth, weaving through a couple of skiers, and then stops to wait for a whole group to pass before leading Barry and me on. Clouds are gathering and the wind is picking up at the top of the mountain. I glance across to the restaurant whilst we wait for these skiers to pass. The building's vast glass front juts out from the mountain. I look to see if Mum and Dad are sat in a window seat watching, but the sky's reflection makes it impossible to see inside.

It doesn't take long to cross that section of the slope. I manage it every time. I don't know why I work myself up into a panic about something I'm capable of doing. I wish I had Ralph's confidence in everything.

I spot the girls as we glide around the bend. They stand to the side of the piste in the heavy snow.

"Is this the place you meant?" Hattie asks Ralph as we pull up.

"Yes, this is it." Ralph plants his ski poles into the deep snow, takes one glove off, pulls up his jacket and fiddles with his transceiver. "So we're going to cut across to Blue 4 from here," he says, very matter of fact, like we've all agreed.

Hattie and Olive are grinning widely.

"I can't wait," squeals Hattie. "It's so exciting."

"Err…off piste?" I question. I didn't sign up for this. My fingers begin to twitch.

"Yeah!" Olive opens her mouth so wide I can see her tonsils. "It's going to be a skiing adventure."

"Ooh!" Barry whistles.

"But we don't have any of the gear like you Ralph," I point out. We can't possibly go.

"Don't worry, it's only just across, between the two pistes. We'll be fine," he tries to reassure me.

We can't even see the other piste from here, let alone our route. What if we hit that rocky patch? I really don't like this idea.

"We promised Mum that we'd stick to 4 and 7," I direct my words at Hattie. I really want that hot chocolate Mum promised and I can't see this being part of the deal.

"Well we are between 4 and 7," whines Hattie. "Come on Barney. You were good on the deep snow remember. Ralph will help us," she puts her arm across Ralph's shoulder and gives him a squeeze.

"Yeah, I'll help you all the way Barney. It'll be fun," Ralph tries to persuade me but I'm nervous. The eyes on my skis seem to be burning a hole in my head. I can feel my pulse racing and the butterflies in my tummy are having a party. All week I've been wanting to prove to Ralph that I am a good skier, but I'm not sure about going off piste.

"You're not scared are you Barney?" sneers Olive. "Come on, I dare you." She flicks her mane of wavy hair out from under her collar. I see red. She's acting really odd, pretending to be so cool. Why does she have to ask me that?

I look out across the deep snow and gulp. Clouds are gathering in the sky, and the tracks aren't as clear as they were from the lift. The silence between us all seems to last forever until Barry quietly speaks out.

"I'm scared coz I'm not as good as the rest of you guys. I'm no ski daredevil. I'm not sure that I can do it." Nobody backs him up. "I think I'd better stay on the piste."

"No worries Barry, I'll stay with you," I quickly decide. "We can finish Red 7, and then race down Blue 4. We'll patrol the slopes and meet you guys where you rejoin the piste on Blue 4. Ralph showed me where the track comes out." A genius bit of quick thinking. "First to the meeting point!"

"We'll be the Ski Patrol Team," Barry spouts excitedly.

Hattie, Olive and Ralph confer.

"Thanks mate," Barry pats me hard on the back and I flinch. "Soz about not being good enough."

"No probs." I won't admit it in front of the others but I'm glad of the excuse. At least Ralph won't find out how bad I am at deep snow.

"Alright then, well we're going," says Hattie defiantly.

"We're the Dare Devils and we'll beat the Ski Patrol Team," teases Olive. I've gone right off her.

Should I tell Hattie not to go? I bet Olive's making her do it. But if I show I'm worried, Olive will probably call me a scaredy cat. She's changed this holiday, and I don't know why I ever had a crush on her. I keep stum.

"Call us if you get stuck, because we all need to go back into the restaurant together. Otherwise we'll get told off for splitting up," instructs Hattie.

That's a deal. I don't want to miss out on that hot chocolate.

"I haven't got my phone," I realise, patting my pockets. "I left it on charge overnight in the room."

"Me neither," says Barry.

Hattie sighs loudly. Unzipping a pocket in her jacket she pulls out her phone. "Take mine, Ralph's and Olive's numbers are in the contacts, you know the code." She makes me feel like a naughty little brother, when I'm not the one doing anything wrong.

"Let's go Dare Devils!" Ralph does a fancy jump into the powder snow and skis away, the girls whooping as they follow. It does look fun.

Barry and I watch for a bit in silence until they disappear amongst a group of trees.

"We'd better get going if we're going to ski down and beat them," I suggest.

"Didn't Ralph say that off piste could be dangerous?" Barry remembers.

"Mm."

CHAPTER 14

DARE DEVILS

As told by Hattie

Look at me, bouncing through the deep snow. My shins are in the front of my boots. The powder is really deep, so I take Ralph's advice to sit back just a little to stop my ski tips digging down too far into the snow. I'm making my own tracks, crossing them with Ralph's ahead of me. We're making patterns in the snow. This is such good fun.

"Woo-hoo!" I cry out. I love it.

I'm not sure what Barney was so worried about. He should be more adventurous. I know he only used Barry as an excuse not to go off piste. He's such a baby sometimes.

Hidden from the piste by the trees it feels like we're venturing into a secret world all alone. I immediately notice the silence that surrounds us. Everything is still whilst we swish through deep snow all by ourselves. It's a tinsy bit frightening but only in an exciting way.

"Ski like a bird swooping through the sky," I sing, making up a song. "Bouncing in the snow, I feel like I can fly. Whoop!"

Bang! I hit something hard beneath the surface. My left ski ricochets off, taking my leg with it. I face plant into the fresh snow.

"You alright?" I hear Ralph calling. His voice is muffled as my head is coated in so much snow.

I feel a bit stunned, it all happened so fast. I'm lying on my front with my right leg bent up in the air behind me, my boot still attached to the ski. I can see my other ski speared like a javelin into the snow to my left.

"Hattie, you alright?" he calls again.

"Err, yeah fine," I splutter, spitting out a lump of snow.

Using my arms I push my body up to sitting. I can hear Olive laughing. What's so funny? I look down towards where the two of them are standing, Olive and Ralph. Why didn't she stop to help me? She was supposed to be skiing behind me. I would've stopped if she had fallen over. I try to ignore them as I brush away the snow from the cuff of my mittens, and around my neck. A trickle of melting ice dribbles down beneath my collar, making me shiver.

"You've got a mountain of snow on top of your helmet!" Olive shouts, still giggling.

I swipe my hand across the top of my head and brush it away. Then I try to move but it's difficult. Swinging my right ski around to sit below me is awkward and it takes a few attempts before I manage to sweep it through the snow. I reach out for my left ski but it's stuck hard, pointing away from me. I try pulling it towards me but it won't budge. How can something as light as a snowflake turn into something so hard as ice. I tug and tug.

"You're pulling it at the wrong angle!" Olive offers me advice. Why doesn't she come and help if she thinks she knows what to do. I thought we were supposed to be a team.

I stretch across to keep wriggling the ski about, but I'm still too far away to do much else.

"You're at the wrong angle," shouts Olive again. "You need to move!"

"Yes I heard you!" I bite back. It's not easy balancing on one ski.

For a minute I sit back down, gather my poles and think about what I can do to get out of this situation. Looking back between the top of the trees I realise I can see a small section of the chair lift in the distance. Typical I fall over on the one part where others can see me. I bet I look rubbish. My eyes are welling up. I don't want to be in the stupid Dare Devils team anymore. Get a grip Hattie, I tell myself. Don't let them see you cry. I sniff, drawing in a big deep breath. Using my pole I push myself up, then take a giant step forward with my left foot and plant it into the deep snow. My boot disappears below the surface, like a foot in sinking sand. Keeping my poles planted in the snow to balance me, I lean away to lever my right ski up in the air and back down beside my left foot. Now with two hands I grab hold of the ski that's speared into a hole. Yanking the ski out, I drop it down beside me. The snow is so fresh that the ski sinks easily creating its own burrow.

"Bash the snow off your boot before you put your ski on!" Olive shouts more orders.

"I know what to do," I grumble. She's just trying to impress Ralph, pretending she's knows everything.

Balancing on one leg, I lift up my left boot to rest it across my other knee. I can see clumps of ice packed onto the sole, so using my ski pole I bash them off. Then I swing my leg back and try to force my boot into the ski, but it won't clip in.

"You might want to check your binding's set," Ralph suggests. Of course he's right, because he does know what he's talking about.

Bending down, I pick up the ski, holding it in one hand and thumping hard on the back binding with my fist until it clicks into position. Carefully, I set the ski down again into the burrow, so as not to spill more snow onto the binding. All this on one leg, I congratulate myself, trying to make me feel better.

Again I kick my boot into the binding but it still won't set. I draw another deep breath, feeling myself shaking as I do.

"Do you want me to come and help you?" Ralph calls up.

I try not to look down at the pair of them in case I start to cry. Instead I twist my ankle across my knee again. There's still a chunk of ice stuck on the heel. How did I miss that? With the pointy end of my pole I dig away until the whole piece flicks off. I stamp my foot back into the binding. Finally I'm ready to go, but I realise I'm still shaking.

"Well done," calls Ralph. "You're doing really well." He makes me feel more confident. "Make your way towards us, just avoid that treetop poking out of the snow."

Olive sniggers, but Ralph doesn't, he's trying to help me.

"Take your time." He keeps talking to me all the way down and I concentrate hard on all the tips he gives me. "Lovely turn Hattie, keep your rhythm going."

I'm so relieved to reach the others. I hate the feeling of being totally alone. Ralph pats me on the back. "Well done," he says. "It was probably a big lump of ice that you hit beneath the surface. You sometimes get those."

"Yeah it was really hard. It all happened so fast."

"You have to ski around them," spouts Olive. What does she know?

"I couldn't avoid it if I didn't know it was there." I'm quick to cut her down.

There's an awkward silence. Maybe I was a bit sharp.

"Sorry," I mumble.

Olive gives me a quick hug. "All safe now and in one piece. Shall we get moving, it's a bit cold standing here."

I'm not cold. I'm very hot and bothered. I fiddle with the zip at the top of my jacket, undoing it a little. Clumps of snow are frozen to my collar.

"Keep close behind me this time, and I promise to stop immediately if you fall again," Ralph assures me.

"Thanks." I still feel a bit shaky after my fall.

Ice trickles down my neck. I'm melting.

CHAPTER 15

SKI PATROL

As told by Barney

"Thanks for staying with me Barney." My friend greets me with a cheesy smile as he plonks himself down onto the chair lift.

"No problem," I reply.

Red 7 is quite short compared with Blue 4. Once we left Hattie and the others at the top, it didn't take us long to reach the chair lift at the bottom. I'm eager to see whether we can spot them off piste. We're going to be in so much trouble if Mum finds out and I bet I'll get the blame for letting Hattie go.

"Barney!" A voice calls out behind us. We turn to see Eve and her elder brother waving as they arrive at the end of the queue.

"Hi!" Barry and I wave back as they shuffle forward. They'll be a couple of chairs behind us.

Her brother is quite a lot older than Eve and is at university. According to Eve, he did a few ski seasons after leaving school, teaching young children to ski, so he must be really good.

"I like it that there's lots of people we know in the resort. Do you?"

"Yeah, it's fun skiing with mates, and playing cards together in the evenings," Barry agrees with me.

I'm not so sure the cards is as much fun. I haven't won a single game yet.

"When we went skiing before with Mum, we didn't know anyone else." I pause. "Apart from Grandpa, he came a few times." Which reminds me I must email him later. I won't tell him about the off piste bit though.

"Does your Grandpa ski?" Barry asks.

"Not now, but he did the first year we came. He helped to teach us."

"Wicked! Wish I had a grandpa who could ski." Barry puts his elbow on the safety bar and rests his chin on his hand.

I didn't say anything else about my family because I know that Barry doesn't really have much himself, not that he talks about anyway.

I scan the side of the piste for a sign of the others. I wonder if they've already dropped over the hill, down the other side or through the trees. I keep looking. Standing out against the white snow I spy a sheer rock face.

"Good job Ralph knows where he's going. Otherwise they'd be in trouble if they came over the top of that," I say to Barry, pointing out the hazard.

"It looks like the kind of place the horrible snowman would live," says Barry.

"Mm." I wish he hadn't mentioned the snowman as I'd managed to forget about it until now.

His shoulders shudder. "Gives me the shivers," he replies.

Misty cloud rolls in across the mountain, the bright sunshine of this morning is quickly disappearing. Picking out the small bumps on the piste is more difficult in this dull light. As the chair lift climbs higher, a freezing wind picks up too, blasting my cheeks. I stop searching for Hattie and turn away from the cold to face my friend.

"I'm over-cooling," says Barry shortly, zipping his jacket up right over his chin.

"Is that the reverse of over-heating? You get too hot with the effort of skiing down the mountain, and then too cold on the chair lift on the way back up."

"Yeah. It's a new term I've made up, over-cooling." He pulls his scarf up over his nose.

We don't speak for a while until Barry blurts out. "Hey Barney, look over there!" He points towards the trees off piste on the far side. I can see a black helmet piled with snow, then the skier brushes it away. The sitting skier gets up. They are wearing yellow salopettes.

"Do you think it's Hattie and she's fallen over?" asks Barry studying the scene. We're thinking the same.

"Certainly looks like it. We could do with a pair of binoculars to know for sure." I squint, cupping my gloves around my face. This wind is vicious up here. "She's moving, so doesn't look like she's hurt."

Barry leans across to take a better look. He lifts up his hand and pretends to be using a telescope. "This is Ski Patrol, I spy Ms Hattie Frank," he speaks in a low, serious tone. "She's lost a ski, it's sticking out of the snow. Oh blimey! Glad I didn't go off piste now, are you?" He elbows me.

"Yeah," I admit. "It takes ages to get the snow off your boots unless Christophe's helping you."

"At least the Dare Devils won't beat us to the meeting point," Barry nudges me again. "We'll be faster than Ralph for once!" He taps a drum roll out on the safety bar.

"Yeah, we'll beat Ralph, we'll beat Ralph," I repeat excitedly.

Hattie disappears behind a couple of trees as the chair lift moves on. We look over our shoulders for a while but we can no longer see her.

Soon the lift arrives at the station on top of the mountain. We slide off the chair and make our way out. In the distance I spot Vijay's black and yellow helmet like a beacon zigzagging down the run.

"Look it's Vijay with his family," I show Barry.

"Yeah I see him, he's difficult to miss," he smiles. We stop a minute whilst Barry adjusts the fastenings on his boots.

We're getting ready to leave, when Eve emerges from the lift station. Barry waves to her and she skis over to where we stand, followed by her very tall brother.

"What were you looking at off the side of the piste?" she asks.

"Did you see?" pipes Barry. "It was…"

"A goat!" I interrupt, bashing Barry on the arm. His face freezes. "It was a mountain goat, trotting through the trees, wasn't it Barry?" I grit my teeth. We mustn't let anyone else know where Hattie is, in case they tell my parents.

"Err…err yeah," he stutters, biting on his bottom lip.

"A goat?" queries Eve.

I nod very quickly up and down, up and down. Eve looks at Barry, who starts to copy me by doing the same fast nodding as if he's my puppet.

"Aren't you skiing with Hattie? I've just seen your mum in the restaurant and she said a group of you were skiing together." Eve is too clever. I think she's sussed us out.

"We are, she's just skied on ahead, so we'd better go," I lie. This is awkward.

"We're skiing Red 7 again. If you're going that way, we can ski together," suggests Eve brightly.

"Sorry, we're meeting on Blue 4." I turn her offer down. I step my skis about to face the direction we need to head off in order to cut across to the right slope.

Eve's smile fades, she's disappointed. I see her shoulders drop as she sighs and feel guilty for not having asked her to join us, but I didn't know we were skiing as a group until Hattie announced it at lunch.

"Perhaps we'll meet you on Blue 4 after your red run. You'll probably catch us up as you're much better skiers than us," I add. "Well done in the race earlier too. I was cheering for you." I think this pleases her.

"Thanks. Might see you later on the blue run." Eve leads her brother away. Effortlessly, she flies off, carving her route down the piste.

"She's as good at skiing as the Secret Assassin," says Barry, gawping at Eve.

"Come on Barry, we'd better get moving."

"Yeah, coz we wanna beat Ralph." Barry boogies away from me, singing as he goes. "Ski Patrol are gonna win, Ski Patrol are gonna win."

CHAPTER 16

TEMPERS

As told by Hattie

I'm not as confident after my fall and my legs are constantly shaking. I need to stop regularly to get my breath back and give my legs a rest. The snow feels heavier and harder to ski through than it did when we started our off piste adventure. The light, flyaway snow at the top has turned into a wet, heavy mush.

We cut into a wood, winding our way through the trees in this winter wonderland. I'm humming to myself when I'm sure I see something flash across a gap between the trees. I don't mention it to the others. The further into the woods we ski, the darker it becomes. I keep having to do snowplough to slow myself down. I'm gripping my leg muscles so hard as I don't want to get left behind in here. Something moves in a branch up above, it startles me. I feel like we're being watched.

All I can hear is my skis scraping through the slush, my own breathing, hot and heavy under my scarf, and the treetop branches swishing in the wind up above. Other than that it's eerily quiet. When I see daylight near the end of the track, my shoulders drop with relief. I don't like the woods.

"Racing on Dare Devils! cries Ralph as he speeds away.

Back out into the open, the snow feels even heavier. My skis won't turn easily and I can't seem to bounce anymore like Christophe taught us. It feels like we're skiing through glue, and every so often my skis get stuck. Hot on my heels I can hear Olive huffing and puffing. I'm struggling to keep up with Ralph, who's obviously more interested in beating Barney than making sure we're OK. Suddenly my skis slip from underneath me, shooting off down the hill. I lose control, opting to crash into the soggy slush before I pick up too much speed.

"Hattie move!" Olive screams.

I tear my arm away from the ground before Olive skis over it, spraying me in splodges of melting snow.

"Wah!" she cries out, failing to turn and tumbling over. Her knees and backside carve a deep hole in the snow. "Hattie that was your fault," she blames me. "You shouldn't have just stopped dead!"

"I didn't stop, I fell over!" I shout back. I make no attempt to get up, so surprised by her reaction. I'm just grateful to still be attached to my skis. At least I haven't lost one again.

Olive brushes down her jacket, shaking lumps of snow out of her pockets.

"It was dangerous to stop like that, I could've hit you." Swinging her skis to run across the mountain, she uses her poles to help her stand. I start to get up too, when suddenly Olive launches another attack. "I'm following Ralph next and you can be out of control at the back."

She skis off to where Ralph is waiting. My mouth drops open. I can't believe she just said that.

"That's it Olive, you are no longer my best friend," I grunt to myself. Shuffling out of the deep hole I've made, I purposely take my time to drop down to where the others stand. I don't care if we lose the race.

Ralph is prodding the snow with his poles, and Olive and I wait in silence, ignoring one another. I wish he'd hurry up, the wind is picking up and it's chilly standing still. Ralph slides his skis across the mountain a few metres ahead and repeats the pole planting.

"Is there a problem Ralph?" I finally ask.

"Um…I think we've gone off course a bit," he says, chewing on his lips. "We need to cut across before we go down any further."

He starts to push away, prowling cautiously like a snow leopard searching for food. We follow like two fighting cubs. I race to get right behind Ralph but Olive leaps into action, quickly skating on her skis to overtake. I pole faster to keep my lead. Ralph stops abruptly and I slide onto the back of his skis until my ski tips crash into his boots and I rebound.

"Aarh," I jar my wrist as my pole catches in the snow. At least it stops me from falling.

"What are you doing?" snaps Ralph, turning his head.

"Sorry." My face scrunches up, my wrist really hurts.

I look to him for sympathy but realise he's staring at Olive, who stops alongside me, a metre lower down.

"She's out of control," barks Olive, shaking her frizzy hair like a poodle.

I frown. Her words sting.

"What are you doing down there?" Ralph growls at Olive. "You should always stay above me. Didn't your instructor teach you anything when you went off piste?"

Olive freezes, taken aback by Ralph's sudden change of attitude. I told Olive not to pretend that we'd been off piste, but she insisted. She said Ralph wouldn't agree to ski with us otherwise.

This could spell trouble. I think we need to be honest with our team leader. We've put all our trust in Ralph, we are totally dependent on him knowing the way.

"We didn't exactly go off piste," I own up. "We were in the deep snow on one side of the run that they hadn't piste bashed."

"What?" he bites back. "Olive, you said you'd both already been off piste."

Olive seems unable to speak. Her mouth keeps opening and closing but nothing comes out. The silence is awkward. I swallow hard. Cracks are opening up, causing a big divide in the Dare Devil team.

"Never go below me, it's dangerous," Ralph instructs, snorting. I flinch. "Please," he says more softly. I think he realises how scary he sounds. "That's why I'm testing the snow to keep us safe," he explains.

Olive nods. I take a few side steps up out of the way so there's space for Olive to slot in behind Ralph, drawing the team back together.

We start to slide forward, none of us talking. Our adventure doesn't feel fun anymore. We don't get far before we hit another problem.

"We'll have to tuck low going down into the dip to get enough speed to take us up the hill the other side." Ralph advises.

I shudder. Speed and heavy snow don't make a good pairing. I've a cold sinking feeling aching in my belly.

Ralph heads off and I tuck down low in his tracks. We race down into the dip and fly up the other side. He slams his skis sideways, braking hard as he reaches the peak. His hand shoots out to signal and he shouts, "STOP!"

I react quickly managing to stop behind him. My heartbeat's racing, I can feel the blood pulsing through my veins. Olive swerves to avoid me, and halts to my left.

"I knew we were too far down." Ralph points to a sharp cliff face rising out of the snow, cutting our route in half. A sheer drop of grey rock drips in jagged icicles. "We need to be up above that ice wall," he points to the rock, his voice is shaking. "We'll have to climb up to the side."

A deep dark hollow hides below the icicles' points. I swear I spy a pair of eyes watching from within, an icy glare just like on Barney's skis. I freeze. "Can you see…"

"We need to get moving," grunts Ralph cutting in. He spreads his skis wide at the front and nearly touching at the back. Leaning forward he plants his poles in either side to help him climb back up the mountain. Olive follows his lead and I tag along behind. I don't mention the eyes again. It's probably just my imagination playing tricks.

I'm not very good at climbing and keep sliding backwards, so I resort to side stepping in order to keep up.

There's a burning in my chest. I'm sweating loads, this is tough. I keep checking that nothing's following us. Olive slides back into my skis a couple of times.

"Ow, grr…," she growls to herself.

I don't moan and she doesn't say sorry either. I guess we both want to get back on track, no time to argue. Ralph storms ahead until he reaches the tip of the cliff face and looks down the other side.

I take a moment to rest whilst Olive sorts her skis out. She's managed to cross them over at the back and they've dug themselves into a groove in the snow. Every time she tries to move the skis just slip back again.

"Grrr, stupid skis," she squeals. Her face is bright pink and she keeps blowing her cheeks out like a puffer fish.

I stick a pole in behind one of her skis to stop it slipping any further. She glances back at me.

"Thanks," I hear her mumble.

Now with one ski stable, she starts to move the other one into fresh snow. I expect she's hoping to get more grip, but the steepness of the slope is making things difficult. "I give up," she groans after another slip backwards.

Moving her skis across the slope to mirror mine, she starts to side step above me. All is quiet as we make our way slowly up the bank. I realise that I can't hear a thing other than the monotonous stepping of our skis. The noise of people on the pistes and the whir of the chair lifts have vanished. We're trapped in a valley between the two runs, and a few flakes start to fall silently from the sky. Looking up at Ralph, I see his blank face. Does he know where we are?

CHAPTER 17

FIRST TO BASE

As told by Barney

Blue 4 seems to go on forever. We wind our way back and forth across the gently sloping piste. I'm leading the way and Barry's close behind. His skiing has massively improved since the start of the week. Snow Patrol are carving out some seriously fast lines. Considering Hattie's already fallen, at this rate, I reckon we're on course for victory against the Dare Devils.

We drop down into the valley where the freezing wind blows against us. On one flat section the wind is so strong that I'm barely moving. Our route bends around the mountain and the wind eases a little on the other side, but then my skillful turns disappear as we hit the wet snow. With this morning's sun having melted the top layer of snow, the run has been carved up by skiers throughout the day. Now it looks more like a mogul field with humps all over the place.

"Woah…, wah…, ugh!" whoops Barry as we negotiate the big bumps.

This is hard work as the wet snow tugs at our skis. Our progress is slow. We stop at the side of piste to check our position.

"There's the bobble hat," I cheer, pointing out a yellow hat with a big pom-pom, stuck on top of a blue stake at the side of the run. "That's where Ralph told me the ski route comes out onto the piste."

Barry peers in the direction of my pointing finger. "Can't see anyone there. We must've beaten them," he grins. "Quick let's get down there before they appear. Ski Patrol go for gold!"

He launches his skis downhill, bouncing his body over the first few small bumps. He swerves to avoid a monstrous mound, clumsily changing his skis from parallel into snowplough, then back to parallel. One leg rises up over a hump as the other cruises around the bottom. Style isn't on Barry's agenda, only winning.

I follow him down and try to catch up with him, but the wet snow seems to keep gripping my skis, holding me back. My knees are aching as I try to perform a series of turns avoiding the obstacles. I'm going slower and slower, but at least I don't fall over.

Eventually we reach the bobble hat and wait.

"We won Barney! I knew we could do it." Barry and I fist pump with our gloved hands. "Champions!"

"Ralph's not gonna like it. That's the second time he's lost to the Frank family today," I chuckle. I feel 'franktastic', bragging rights are allowed this evening and I'm looking forward to it.

We continue waiting for what feels like ages. I watch the chair lift slowly disappear into the cloud covering the mountain top. Mist rolls down the hillside towards us. I scour the off piste for signs of life but spot nothing. The mountains rise sharply either side of the piste. I guess Hattie and the others must be hidden in a gully. I wonder if they came past the mountain hut route.

"What's the time?" I ask Barry.

He sticks his poles in the ground and tugs at the sleeve of his jacket, trying to check his watch. "Err...it's just gone three twenty," he replies.

"Come on Hattie," I mumble. "We promised Mum we'd be back by three thirty. We need to get on that chair lift pronto." Scanning the hillside, hoping for the three of them to make an appearance, I start to worry.

"You don't think they've gone up without us do you?" Barry suggests.

"Nah, we said meet on the piste, didn't we?" I'm starting to doubt myself. What if someone moved the bobble hat? I look around, there are definite tracks joining the piste here.

"Yeah, I think so." We wait a while longer, both of us watching out for skiers to appear, then Barry suggests "why don't you try calling Ralph?"

"Good idea," I agree. I pull off one glove and unzip the pocket of my jacket to find Hattie's phone. It starts snowing a few small flakes.

I'm punching in the code when Barry starts waving like mad.

"Yoo-hoo!" he hoots.

"What are you doing?" I glance up whilst scrolling through Hattie's contacts list. "Can you see them? Where are they?" I can't see anyone off the side of the piste.

"No," he replies.

Ralph's face pings up on the screen, I press the 'call' button.

"Yoo-hoo! Eve over here," Barry hollers.

"Oh no," I groan. My mouth stays open, I hold the phone to my ear, mesmerised by the green figure bobbing down the mountain out of the mist. She flies towards us through the wet snow without any problem at all. How does she make it look so effortless?

"Hi," she says as she slides up beside me. "Haven't you found Hattie?"

No one is answering the phone. Now I'm gawping at Eve. She skis so fast, I've had little time to think.

"No, we reckon she must've gone a different route," I lie. Pick up the phone, Ralph, please pick up the phone. The words spin about inside my head. "Where's your brother?" I ask trying to divert her attention.

"He's going up on the chair lift for one last run but my leg is sore so I'm heading in. I've had enough for today," she replies.

"We beat Hattie and the others to the meeting point." Barry's shoulders dance about as he shuffles his skis excitedly. I cough loudly and shake my head to stop him talking but he carries on, not understanding my signals. "Ski Patrol have beaten the Dare Devils. We won, we beat Ralph."

"Ralph?" Eve queries.

The phone is still ringing. My eyes dart from Barry to Eve.

"Yeah, he took Hattie and Olive on a short cut off piste," blurts Barry without thinking.

"Off piste?" Eve sounds alarmed.

"Oops!" Barry sucks his lips in, sealing his mouth shut.

"Sorry I can't take your call right now," the recorded message blasts out of the phone.

I cut the call.

CHAPTER 18

THE CRASH

As told by Hattie

Olive stands aside, letting me go behind Ralph. I think it's her way of saying sorry. I'm sorry too. I don't really want to fall out with my best friend.

The snow is horrible. It's so wet and clings to my skis. Large chunks of ice litter our route making it tricky to avoid a collision. I can't control my skis very well in these conditions.

Skiing between the two pistes is taking longer than I expected. After another three or four short turns Ralph stops. He prods the snow. He pushes on then repeats the same exercise again and again. As we stand waiting for him to decide which way to go, I glance back up towards the woods, but there are several clumps of trees and in this grey light I'm not even sure which route we took. Much higher up and further over than we have travelled, I spy a run-down old hut hiding in the trees. Why would anyone build a hut there, I wonder?

"There's an old…," I begin.

"This way," growls Ralph tracking back across the mountain taking a new route.

"I think we should stay quiet and do as he says," Olive advises me in a low voice.

I sigh. I'm not even sure he knows what he's prodding for anymore. We move on, our direction changing once again.

Fog now hugs the mountaintop. Where did the sun go? It's much more difficult to see the lumps in the snow in this grey light. Mountain weather changes so fast, and I think the temperature's dropped too. I'm beginning to get cold since we're now going so slowly.

"How far to go?" Olive calls from the back.

"Not far, I think we're nearly there," replies Ralph, his voice shaking. Is he cold too?

We dip into a hollow, walls of snow climbing up around us. Lines are scratched into the surface as if a giant bear has clawed at it, dragging down a series of mini-avalanches. We carry on navigating our way through the battered balls of ice. I listen out for the whir of a chair lift, or the noise of other people on a piste, but I still can't hear anything. Perhaps everyone's gone back to their hotels for the day since the weather is getting worse. Large snowflakes swirl about in the wind.

We pause again as we come across a really steep part. I turn to Olive, hoping for some reassurance, but I can see she's twitching nervously too. Peering ahead, she lets out an obvious sigh as Ralph starts his snow poking routine. Wiping her mitten against her cuff, she pulls up her sleeve to look at her watch.

"It's nearly three thirty!" she barks.

"Oh no, we're going to be late. I hope Barney's still waiting," I worry aloud. Mum is going to kill me if she finds out where we've been.

"Ralph do you actually know what you're doing?" Olive questions.

Ralph bristles, he stands up straight and doesn't turn around.

"Yes!" he bites back. "I just missed the track that's all. If you two hadn't been competing all the time, I might've been able to concentrate."

"Huh!" Olive pouts, clouds of hot air stream from her nostrils. She's sulking.

I think Ralph may have a point. I feel embarrassed that we were squabbling. It was fun at the top when we first left the piste, but it's not much fun now.

"You said you knew the way," moans Olive.

"I do!" Ralph is growing more irritable. Olive's whining is winding him up now. I think I should back Ralph since he's the only one who can get us out of here, but I'm not sure what to say.

"You don't know where we are," squeals Olive. I spin round urging her to shh. She drums her ski poles into the snow, her face all screwed up. I can't tell whether she's angry or frightened. "We're lost!"

My ski tips hang over the edge of a hair-raising drop. I daren't lean too far forward to look for fear of falling away. Oh help, I've never done anything as steep as this before.

"We're not lost," Ralph retaliates, his glare hidden by his mirrored goggles. His head flicks back to face downhill.

"Follow me!" he cries, launching off at speed down the sheer face.

Tears well in my eyes. Thump, thump, thump, my heart is beating so fast in my chest. As I take a deep breath and drop away after him, my stomach flies up into my mouth. I gulp. My knees are bent with a small gap between them, just like Ralph's. They take a battering as we hit an icy patch without snow. My skis scrape across the surface until they fall back into the slush. The change of speed jolts my body but I manage to stay upright. Back onto ice, Ralph zooms ahead, I fly after him, my body rigid with fear. I hear Ralph's phone blast out loud. His hand lifts up but as he reaches across his chest, his ski tips cross and his body jolts forward. One ski is yanked out to the side, spinning his body around as his boot breaks free. I jump at an angle across the mountainside, slamming both ski edges into the snow to avoid a collision. I crouch as my knees bang together, my skis scraping over the ice as I try to stop. I can hear Olive doing the same close behind me. Out of control on one ski and going backwards, Ralph's remaining boot flicks out of the other binding and he tumbles over and over again. It all happens so fast.

"Aarh!" he yells and yells, until finally he hits deep snow. His body stops falling and he lies crumpled in a heap. Everything goes silent, as if time has frozen.

CHAPTER 19

WHERE ARE THEY?

As told by Barney

Eve leans forwards, her jaw dropping open. "Hattie, Ralph and Olive are off piste?" she repeats slowly.

Barry hangs his head. "Forget I said that," he says quietly.

"Just the three of them?" She prods for more information.

I don't speak and neither does Barry anymore. I'm grateful for my dark goggles. Hopefully Eve can't see the fear in my eyes. I've got one eye on Eve and the other scanning the off piste, willing Hattie to appear.

"The three of them on their own," she states. I gulp, slowly giving her one nod to confirm her suspicions. "Without a guide?" she guesses.

"Um…" I don't know what to say. I feel stupid for lying to her before. Obviously, she now knows they've gone off piste, alone.

Her head moves back away from me, as she takes it all in. Her helmet twists to the side like a robot as she scans the off piste, but the visibility is very poor. I dread to think what the mountain is like over the first hillock and into the trees. I rack my brains trying to picture what it looked like earlier when Ralph first showed me the exit route. I didn't pay enough attention. I didn't realise it would be so critical.

It's gone half past three now. Mum's going to be wondering where we are. What if something's happened to Hattie? I shouldn't have let her go, but it was her choice. I start to feel a bit sick.

"How long have they been gone Barney?" Eve calmly asks. I feel I can trust Eve. It's not like she's telling me off, I think she wants to help.

"Half an hour, maybe a bit longer, possibly an hour."

"We left them on the red run, where the run splits in two," Barry explains. "Not long before we saw you at the top."

Eve nods. "I know where you mean. We went off piste there with our guide."

"So Ralph will know the way," I check, this sounds positive. Perhaps they are just taking their time.

"I doubt he'll know it well enough, not in this weather," Eve sighs.

Snow is falling heavily now. I watch it sticking to Eve's goggles and melting around her face. Her long eye lashes are blinking until her green eyes glare at me, like cat's eyes in the dark.

"Trouble is, there are a few steep drops you need to avoid in order to get all the way across." She bites on her bottom lip.

"Couldn't they just go straight across if they can't see well enough? They'd just come out a bit further up. Maybe we missed them," Barry suggests hopefully.

"Not really, depends on the snow. It's been warm all morning, so there's more risk of an avalanche in the afternoon. Were they coming via the hut?" she asks me.

"Ralph did mention a hut, he pointed it out to me when we were on the chair lift," I remember.

"Wait here." She climbs up the small step into the deep snow and poles along the tracks made by other skiers.

Reaching a small hill, she side steps up it to look over the top. Her helmet swivels as she scans the area.

"What are we going to do?" Barry asks. "Do you think they're in trouble?" He pushes his fingers into his cheeks making his face look really chubby.

My mouth fills with saliva. "I've no idea." My voice is weak. I'm dead worried.

Eve returns, sliding along the tracks already cut into the deep snow.

"I can't see any sign of them. Did the girls have rucksacks and transceivers?" asks Eve.

I shake my head. I'd never even heard of a transceiver before today. I grip Hattie's phone in my hand. "She hasn't even got her phone," I whisper.

"Try phoning Ralph again," Barry taps the phone clasped in my hand.

I input the code number. Ralph's picture and number appear on the screen. My hand is shaking from the cold as I press dial and loudspeaker.

All three of us lean in to listen. The phone rings and rings and rings, but no one picks up.

CHAPTER 20

BROKEN

As told by Hattie

Skis and poles litter the snow. I grab the poles, which landed not too far from me, and carefully drop down to where Ralph lies. He hasn't moved since his fall. Olive, with her own skis still facing across the steep slope, side-slips down to collect up both of Ralph's skis. The tip of one ski appears to have split apart from the base. The two parts clatter together as she makes her way down. Mounds of wet mushy snow build up on her skis as she edges towards us.

"Ralph," I bend down, resting a hand on his shoulder as he lies on his side in the snow. He winces and I immediately lift my hand off. "Ralph are you OK?"

He's sniffing with short sharp breaths. I guess he's trying to be brave, as he's not crying but his face is so pale. He doesn't move his body or his legs, preferring to lie still as he landed on the snow.

"Where does it hurt?" I ask, realising that he's clearly in pain. Gently his hand taps his lower leg, the one that's bent up in front of him.

Olive arrives with Ralph's skis. "Here you go?" she says, laying them down below him. "I found this too." Her nose wrinkles and her mouth twists up as if she's sucking a sour chew. Bending down she presents Ralph with his phone, the glass smashed like crazy paving. "I don't think it's working anymore."

Ralph doesn't bother taking the phone. In fact I don't think he's listening to a word Olive's saying. His pale face looks almost green, as he lies there immobile. He groans. I hope he's not going to be sick. Olive flinches away, quickly standing up. She grabs a handful of her red hair, pulling it forward to hide her horrified face. Her green eyes focus on mine.

"What are we going to do?" she whispers.

CHAPTER 21

PICK UP

As told by Barney

"Try phoning Olive," Eve suggests.

I start scrolling through the contacts, but my fingers are so cold and snow keeps landing on the phone so it won't react to my fingerprint. The weather is closing in and big snowflakes are raining down on us. The visibility is getting bad too, I'm even struggling to see the chair lift.

"Here, dry your hand and the phone on this," Eve passes me a tissue from her pocket. "I'll hold my hands here to keep the phone dry." She cups her gloves above the phone providing a canopy to stop the snow falling on it.

I do as she suggests and manage to find Olive in the contacts list. I press dial and wait for someone to answer.

The phone rings and rings. Please answer the phone Olive. It's getting colder. I realise my hand holding the phone is shaking too. We've been stood at the side of the piste for so long now.

"Hi," a voice speaks.

"Olive!" I call out. My shoulders sink in relief. "Olive, where…"

"I can't get to the phone right now," the voice cuts in, "so leave a message after the beep and I'll get back to you."

My jaw locks. The phone beeps. I can't speak.

Eve reacts quickly and dives to the rescue. "Olive, this is Eve. Call us back on Hattie's phone urgently." The line cuts off. I'm grateful that Eve seems to be taking charge. My mind is in chaos.

"We need to tell someone," Eve decides. She appears to know just what to do. "Phone your mum, you must let her know what's going on. I'll phone my brother and instructor to raise the alarm, they'll be able to organise an emergency search."

"My mum!" Now I feel really sick and I need the loo. I don't feel grateful or glad anymore. Instead I'm full up with dread.

Barry lifts up his goggles, resting them against his helmet. "An emergency search?" he asks, his big brown eyes light up. "This is serious stuff, isn't it? An SOS, a proper distress signal." His voice goes all deep, and his eyes dart back and forth between me and Eve. "Are the Dare Devils in real danger?"

"They could be," Eve warns.

Barry fixes his stare upon Eve. He pings his goggles back onto his face. "How can I be of assistance?"

I'm surprised he doesn't salute her.

"You can call my mum." I slap the phone into his palm.

CHAPTER 22

RINGING

As told by Hattie

'Quack, quack, quack.' Olive's phone bursts into life ringing from within her jacket.

"Quick answer it!" I urge her.

In a flap, she fiddles with the zip on her top pocket. It jams. I reach across and try to tug it for her but it won't budge. 'Quack, quack, quack,' the phone rings. She rips off her gloves, dropping them on the snow.

"You hold the top and I'll hold the bottom," she suggests.

Pulling the zip taught at each end, we manage to open the pocket. Olive grabs the phone as it stops ringing.

"It was your phone!" she says in alarm, staring at me. "Your phone was calling me."

"Barney," I reply. "I gave my phone to Barney remember. He'll be trying to call us. Call him back, we need to get help."

Her fingers tap on the phone. I look down at Ralph lying with his helmet resting on the floor. His mouth is drooping and his nose is running.

I bend down and say softly to him, "don't worry Ralph, we're going to call for help."

Even without being able to see his eyes, he still looks so sad. We need to get help quickly.

"Is it ringing?" I turn my attention back to Olive.

She takes the phone away from her ear, pushes her goggles up onto her helmet and taps again. Snow is sticking to her beautiful wavy hair like a heavy frosting. Snowflakes melt onto her face and run down her cheeks. Then I realise that her eyes are beginning to well up. Her lips roll together keeping her mouth firmly closed.

"Olive?" I question.

A giant, bulbous teardrop runs down her cheek.

"I've run out of charge," she weeps. "What are we going to do?"

I feel colder than I've ever felt before. Like all the heat is draining from my body.

CHAPTER 23

OFF PISTE

As told by Barney

Barry thrusts the phone against my ear.

"Err, hi Mum," I feel out of breath.

"Barney, is that you?" I hear Mum questioning on the other end of the line.

I lick my lips and try to swallow. "Yeah," I croak.

"What's going on? You're late. Why is Barry phoning me from Hattie's phone? He says you've got something to tell me. Have you gone back to the hotel? Because we are waiting for you up here. Your father's moaning about his aching muscles. I really think he needs to go back down in the cable car and get in a hot bath." She barely pauses for breath. "And if you don't get here soon, the cable car will stop running and he'll have to ski down, and that will take forever. He's making such a fuss. I knew we should've arranged for you to come back sooner. You forget how long it takes queuing for lifts. Are you on the lift now?"

"No. I'm near the bottom of Blue 4," I tell her, which is exactly where I am.

"Bottom of Blue 4. Right, well there's no point in you coming back up here. Make your way back to the hotel and we'll meet you there. I'll get Dad in the cable car," she's spouting orders and I don't want to interrupt. "Olive's mum has been getting worried. Her dad doesn't seem so bothered, but he's had a few too many glasses of wine if you ask me. I'll let her mum know that you're heading back to the hotel. Ok darling…"

"No, Mum, don't do that," I finally summon the courage to speak.

"What?" she hesitates briefly. "Why not?" I don't normally tell my mum what to do.

I gulp hard. "Because Olive isn't with us, nor is Hattie," I say clearly. I may sound calm but I certainly don't feel it. In fact, I feel faint. I lean against Barry for support.

"What do you mean they're not with you?" The tidal wave is building momentum and I have a feeling I'm about to feel its full force. Very slowly she asks, "where are they?"

Barry's ear is stuck to mine, listening in to the conversation. He nudges me. "Tell her they're with Ralph," he whispers.

"Is that Barry? What did he say?"

I swallow again, trying to wet my dry mouth. "They're with Ralph."

"Where with Ralph?" Her voice is very serious now, she's gone into teacher mode.

"I don't know exactly," my voice is trembling.

"What's going on?" I can hear Dad asking in the background.

Voices become muffled. I reckon Mum's got her hand across the receiver. Then I think I hear Mum say, "Get Olive's parents, quick."

"Barney," says Mum, her voice clear again. Then incredibly calmly she asks, "where do you think they might be?"

"Somewhere between Blue 4 and Red 7," I pause to build up courage.

"Tell her," Barry eggs me on.

"Between Blue 4 and Red 7," Mum repeats, half questioning.

"Yes." I take a deep breath and blurt out, "off piste."

"OFF PISTE! OFF PISTE!" I hold the phone away from my ear and can still hear Mum screeching. She's not calm anymore.

CHAPTER 24

EMERGENCY ACTION

As told by Hattie

Olive stands beside Ralph, hands on her hips, looking down at him in despair.

"We need to keep Ralph warm," I tell her.

"We need to go for help," she replies, shaking her head, disagreeing with me.

"We can't go for help, we don't know where we are." Ralph was our leader, neither Olive nor I have been off piste before. We've no idea what to do. The snow is falling so fast now, you can barely see 20 metres ahead. I feel like I'm in a snow globe that's been heavily shaken.

"How's anyone going to find us if they don't know where we are?" she snaps. "We can't wait here all night. We'll go together and find help."

"No, we can't leave Ralph," I stand firm.

"We have to try," she disagrees, scooping up her gloves and yanking them onto her hands.

"We're lost!" I cry out. "You said so yourself. In fact, if you hadn't shouted at Ralph earlier, then he might not have dropped off the cliff so fast and fallen over."

"It's not my fault he fell over," she shouts back. "He tried to answer his phone. He wasn't concentrating. I bet it was your brother calling him." She's waggling her pointy finger at me.

"My brother. You can't blame it on my brother!"

"Girls," Ralph moans weakly, still holding onto his leg. He takes his helmet off, discarding it in the snow. Drained and in agony he pleads with us, "please stop arguing." It's the most he's spoken since crashing.

I drop onto my knees beside Ralph, leaving Olive standing. Hot breath steams out of her nostrils as she snorts.

"Please don't leave me," Ralph mutters. He sounds very small and very weak. He's shivering, his teeth chattering as he speaks. I rest my hand gently on his shoulder.

Olive unclips her bindings. She picks up her skis, walks away from Ralph and digs her skis into the ground above him, making a cross shape. Carefully she moves back to kneel down the other side of him.

"I've made a warning sign. Mine are the brightest patterned skis, hopefully someone will spot them. Hattie's right, we need to stick together. We won't leave you Ralph," she sniffs. Olive looks across at me, tears streaming down her cheeks, but she wipes them away, hiding her face from Ralph. "How should we keep him warm?"

I reach out and touch her arm. She smiles, bravely holding back the sobs just like I am.

I help Ralph to put his helmet back on to stop him losing any more heat from his head. We clear away the snow that collected in the collar of his open jacket as he fell. Olive is wearing two scarves. She unwraps one and ties it around Ralph's neck, tucking it down inside his jacket, which we zip up to the top. The way he has fallen makes it awkward for us both to lay beside him. He's currently lying on his side and we don't want to move him in case we damage his leg even more. He says that his head and body are comfortable. After thinking about it all, we remove his rucksack from his back and lay it across his chest to act as an extra barrier to the snow. Then we take it in turns to lie against his back, hugging him with our arms. Every so often we rub his arm and shoulder, trying to warm both him and us.

Rummaging through the rucksack I realise that Ralph carries a pouch full of water. I find the straw attached to the tank and feed it to Ralph. He takes little sips, and Olive and I take a drink too. I also find an extra fleece and a torch in the rucksack. We stuff the fleece down inside his jacket, wrapping it around his body. I hold the torch in my hand.

"I'll keep this out, so we can shine it as it gets dark." Olive nods in agreement, her yellow goggles glowing in the grey light. "Barney's probably already raised the alarm. Help will be here soon." I try to convince the others. I really hope he has, but what if he's too scared to tell?

Every minute we are out here, the heavier the snow falls, the colder we become, and the darker the day grows. I wish I could turn back time to when we were standing at the top of the piste. I should have taken the same route as Barney and Barry. I should've taken the red run. I went off piste because Olive wanted to go and Ralph was keen too. I had a choice and I made the wrong decision.

I brush a layer of snow off the patient's arm. The flakes are sticking fast, quickly building up along Ralph's legs.

I want to be back at the hotel. I want to have a steaming hot bath. I want to be wrapped up in my pjs and a dressing gown, sat on the bed watching TV. I want to be cuddling my mum.

CRACK! We all jump. Olive and I sit up, scanning the area. My pulse is racing so fast, I'm sure I can hear it in my ears.

"It came from the woods," whispers Olive.

Scared rigid, we focus on the trees. What or who was that?

CHAPTER 25

PANIC

As told by Barney

Barry leans back as my mum's voice rants out of the phone and it's not even on loudspeaker. "What were you thinking Barney, letting her go? Get Olive's parents quick!" she orders Dad. "Crickey, what are we going to do?" I haven't spoken for a while. What can I say? "We need to alert someone, it's going to be dark soon."

Eve grabs the phone from me.

"Mrs Frank, it's Eve here. I've phoned my brother and my instructor who are going to start a search along with Christophe."

"That's my instructor Mum," I butt in.

Eve continues, "I've explained exactly where Hattie and the others left the red run and where they were expecting to rejoin the blue run. Christophe will alert the emergency team in the resort to get their help. I've passed them both Ralph's and

Olive's phone numbers so they can track the last known position of the phones, and Ralph should be wearing a transceiver." Eve is dead calm and organised. She appears to know exactly what to do.

I can hear Mum relaying this information to Dad and Olive's parents.

"But Olive's never been off piste before!" says an alarmed, high-pitched voice which I guess is Olive's mum's. Should I point out that Hattie has never been off piste either?

Then I hear Dad calling out to someone else. "Have you heard what's happened? Your son has taken my daughter and Olive off piste!"

I hold my glove over my mouth. "They're arguing!" I whisper to my friends. Eve's eyes pop out and Barry's lips blow out a long hiss.

Dad is ranting in the background. Everyone is suddenly talking at once; it's difficult to hear what anyone is saying.

"Calm down, calm down!" I make out Mum telling Dad. "Hattie chose to go. For all we know, it may have been her idea." I'm glad Mum said that because thinking back, the girls seemed very keen and excited to go. They may well have talked about it together and got Ralph to agree to take them.

"Where are they now?"

"Ralph's father," I mouth to the others. I can recognise his deep voice, he sounds like a sergeant major. You wouldn't argue with Ralph's father. He's very strict, according to Ralph.

"Lost!" Dad snaps. That's not exactly helpful.

"Somewhere between Red 7 and Blue 4. Christophe the instructor is heading there now," Mum explains.

"I've been on the route off piste with Ralph before, I know it well. My son is wearing a transceiver so we may be able to pick up a signal." We hear the secret assassin say.

"I hope Ralph turned his transceiver on," whispers Eve.

"He did, he definitely did, I saw him do it before they left us," I reply.

She covers the mouthpiece with her gloves. "Good but it'll only help once they are close enough to be in range."

"Here, can you take my younger son back to the hotel with you? I only collected him from Christophe about 15 minutes ago," Ralph's dad continues. "I'll head out to find Christophe and help in the search."

"Yes," I hear both Mum and Olive's mother agree, "yes of course."

"Here's my card, it's got my mobile number on it. Keep in touch. I'll call you as soon as we find them."

"Thanks," says Dad. "Sorry I had a go at you." I'm glad Dad is apologising. I guess he shouted earlier because he is so worried about the danger Hattie could be in and he thinks it's Ralph's fault, but I'm not so sure.

"There's no need to apologise. I'll be as angry with Ralph as anybody. Let's just get them back safe." The Secret Assassin sounds so calm. He's already worked out a plan and he's putting it into action.

Conditions are worsening and the light is fading. I hope they find them soon. I'm shivering in the snow as the three of us huddle over the phone.

"Mrs Frank?" Eve speaks into the phone. "Mrs Frank?"

"Yes, Eve, sorry, we were just organizing," says Mum.

They've barely done any organising. Eve's arranged most of it. All they did was panic and shout at each other.

Eve leans over the phone.

"I will go back to the hotel now with Barney and Barry. It's getting very cold out here and the lifts are about to close. I think you need to get to the cable car soon."

"Oh my gosh, look at the time. We need to get the cable car down, quickly," Mum talks to the parents. "Barney," she barks back down the phone, "we'll meet you in the hotel lounge."

I'm not looking forward to that meeting.

CHAPTER 26

RESOURCEFULNESS

As told by Hattie

Olive and I stare into the woods for ages but see or hear nothing.

I feel weak and my tummy keeps rumbling. I dig about in my pocket for the small bar of chocolate I hid in there this morning. Ralph appears to be asleep and I'm not sure whether an injured person should be given food. I tear the wrapper open and break the bar in two, offering half to Olive.

"Thanks," whispers Olive, taking the chocolate from my hand. "Sorry I shouted at you earlier."

"I'm sorry we argued too. Stupid really, us arguing in an emergency situation," I sort of laugh.

"Yeah, daft." Olive rolls her eyes.

My throat is sore, we've both been shouting for what seems like ages, trying to attract attention, but no one's heard us. The silence is creepy. It's difficult to see much past the trees now because of the snow and mist. I keep imagining pairs of eyes looking at me from the darkness of the woods. What if the Abominable Snowman really does exist? I edge closer to Olive.

"I'm getting cold too now. Are you?"

She wraps her arms across her own body and rubs. Because we've stopped moving around, our bodies are cooling down. I lean across and slide her goggles back down onto her face.

"Keep your goggles on, at least they'll keep your face dry," I suggest. She nods back at me.

The snowfall has been heavy for a while now and a layer of snow has stuck to Ralph's salopettes. We keep brushing it off of his arm and body but we daren't touch his legs as that's where he feels pain.

I did think about ripping off a few branches from the fir trees and trying to make some kind of cover. That's what they do in survival programmes, I'm sure of it. Only that'd mean going into the woods where the eyes lurk. The more I think about it, the more I feel like we're being watched.

"Why don't we swap over for a bit?" I croak, my throat is so sore. "You can get up and do a few star jumps to warm up." Besides, I prefer to stay put next to Ralph. That way I'm not looking at the eyes.

Olive gets up and jogs on the spot. I stuff the chocolate wrapper back in my pocket, jamming my finger into something else. I start pulling out a long thread.

"Olive," I hold up my find to show her, "look what I've found."

Her eyes light up.

CRACK!

Olive and I both jump up this time. For a second I lose my breath.

"What was that?" croaks Ralph.

CRACK! An almighty crash thunders out of the woods as several large branches plunge to the ground.

"Phew!" I gasp. The relief makes me want to laugh. "Just branches breaking under the weight of all the snow," I say.

"We need to get those branches." Olive grabs my arms.

"What?" She must be joking, I am not going anywhere near those woods.

"We can use them as a shelter from the snow. Come on!" She drags me away, without waiting for me to agree. "We have to be quick."

Stumbling through the deep snow, we run towards the trees. I concentrate on the branches and try not to think about the eyes. My mouth is dry, I'm desperate for more water. As we reach the perimeter, Olive grabs the first branch.

"Get that one," she orders, directing me to one just inside the first line of trees.

Cautiously I tiptoe into the woods murmuring, "please don't eat me, please don't eat me."

I reach out for the big branch, its end spiky where it has split from the trunk. Not stopping to look around, I drag the fronds behind me, leaping across the snow to return to Ralph as soon as possible.

"Don't look back," I chant to myself.

CHAPTER 27

WAITING

As told by Barney

"What's going on?" Vijay races out of the lift as soon as we cross through the lobby. "My mother says Hattie and Olive are lost." Word travels fast. "Where did they go? I can't believe I've missed all the action."

I find it difficult to speak as my teeth are chattering.

"Come, come children, let's get you in front of the fire in the lounge," says Vijay's mum ushering us out of the lobby. "I'll order some hot chocolate and cake to warm you up." She taps Vijay on the head. "We need to look after your friends Vijay, not interrogate them," she warns him.

Eve's parents race over and wrap their daughter in their arms as soon as we walk into the lounge. I know it's not my fault, yet I can't help feeling guilty, especially now that Christophe and Eve's brother are out there searching. It's not only Hattie and my friends who are in danger but the rescuers too. They risk their own lives to save others. I've never really thought about it before.

Eve's parents are helping coordinate the search and are in regular contact with the rescue team. Vijay's mum walks back from the bar with hot drinks and cake. I feel comforted to have some adults looking after us whilst we wait for my parents to return. They are all so kind.

Sitting beside the roaring fire, Vijay searches the internet on his dad's laptop. I watch the flames flickering, the glow of the burning log warming my cheeks. I lean against the soft woolly cushion. My eyes feel sleepy but my brain is wide awake, going over and over my lift journey with Ralph.

"Look I've found some photos and a map of the routes people take between the two pistes." He turns the screen to face me. I notice that he skips any dramatic drops or cliff-edge pictures. Instead he's keen to show me smiling skiers having fun.

"Wait." I pull his hand off the mouse-pad. "That's the mountain hut, in the trees. Ralph pointed it out to me.

"This could be useful info," he says, whisking the laptop away. Vijay runs over to Eve and her parents, showing them the photo. There's a lot of nodding. I sigh, Eve already knows about the hut. I wish I could remember what else Ralph had said.

I stare into the blizzard but can barely make out the difference between the off piste and the blue run in the dim light. My eyes are glued to the spot where we stood waiting for Hattie. I cup the mug of hot chocolate in my hands, though I still feel cold deep inside. Where are you Hattie?

***

There's a lot of commotion in the lobby as my parents arrive back at the hotel. I've got goosebumps as I see them walk through the archway into the lounge. I set my mug down on the tiled table. The three of us stand up, Barry, Vijay and me, not sure how to react. Mum walks swiftly across the room, her salopettes brushing together as she hurries. She puts an arm around first me, and then Barry, giving us both a big squeeze.

"Thank goodness you two are safe," she weeps. Then she moves across to Eve, hugging her tightly. "And you my darling girl, you are amazing."

Vijay looks on expectantly. "I've been helping with the computer," he informs Mum. His big eyes glistening in the lights. A blank stare is all she's giving. This is awkward. "I've photos of the route," he holds the screen up for her to see, touching the mouse-pad by accident as he tries to show her the smiling skiers. Mum puts a hand to her chest. Vijay glances back at the screen. "Oops sorry not that one," he quickly removes the jumping skier dropping off a cliff face. Cool photo but not one for Mum right now.

Olive's dad walks up and nods to us. For some reason I offer out my hand to shake. He grasps it in both hands, gripping it tightly. I thought he'd never leave go.

"Good job lad," he says. "Good job."

What did I do? I don't feel like I've done anything worth praising. Olive's mum stands at the window staring into space. I should've persuaded their daughter not to go off piste, but I was too annoyed about her showing off in front of Ralph. Was I jealous?

Dad limps in. "Alright son," he embraces me and pats Barry on the back. "Well done for raising the alarm," he says. I wish I felt relieved but without any word of Hattie, I feel broken.

Ralph's mum runs into the bar in her dressing gown and a white towel wrapped around her head. Her face is plastered in white cream, with two holes around her eyes. I have to stop myself from giggling.

"I've just had a call from my husband about the children," she cries dramatically, holding the back of her hand to her forehead. I bet she's an actress or something equally glamorous, to be married to the Secret Assassin. "They still haven't found them. He says they are close to the tracker's signal but still no sign. And the conditions are awful!" she wails. She squeezes hold of Ralph's little brother.

All the mothers huddle together and comfort one another.

What if Hattie and Olive made Ralph take them off piste? Maybe he wanted me to go to help out, or perhaps he was hoping I'd persuade the girls not to go at all. I did neither. I took the easy option and hid behind Barry's strength, the only one of us big enough to admit that he didn't want to go. I stuck by my teammate but created a split with the others.

I feel dreadful. All this emotional stuff is exhausting.

CHAPTER 28

WHISTLE

As told by Hattie

"If you need me just whistle." That's what Grandpa said when he gave me the whistle on our first ever trip to the Lake District, walking up mountains. "Water, whistle, map, compass, a torch and a few supplies," he'd reel off the list as he was packing his rucksack, making sure the Kendal Mint Cake was near the top. The whistle had been in my pocket ever since.

"At least I remembered the whistle Grandpa," I mutter to myself, holding it in my hand, the lanyard around my neck.

I blow it for what seems like forever. Olive has a go too. We stand up and pace around Ralph blowing the whistle in all directions but no one hears. At least our fir-tree canopy is working well and is protecting us from the snow. We both duck back under it. I find some hand-warmer pouches in my pockets too, so I bend and flex the plastic until they start to generate some heat, then I tuck one inside Ralph's jacket. He's fallen asleep.

"What if no one comes to find us before it's too late?" Olive sobs. "It's all my fault, I wanted it to be exciting. Nothing like this was meant to happen. I'm sorry," she cries. "I'm so sorry." Her words are drowned out by her sobbing.

"Don't cry Olive," I try comforting her. "All three of us made the decision to do it."

Going off piste was Olive's idea and Ralph was reluctant at first. Maybe he knew we shouldn't really go alone, but Olive had been persistent. I don't think she understood the dangers. It was easy to get swept along by her excitement. I thought it sounded like fun and daring. Any one of us should've been bold enough to say no, yet none of us did.

I manage to calm her down, getting her to lay quietly next to Ralph, her sniffs shuddering as her sobs subside.

Ralph is wheezing as he sleeps. He looks so peaceful hiding under the branches. I tuck myself in next to Olive. The wind howls through the trees as we curl up close together. The snowflakes keep falling silently, white like the feathers of a thousand swans, gradually covering our canopy. We're alone, in the middle of nowhere, with just trees, rocks and snow for company. It's spooky. Our shelter shivers in the wind. What if the snow covers us completely and we can't be seen? Maybe we should stick all the skis in the ground to mark where we are hiding. Anything coloured in a world of white should stand out. When will help come? Will it come at all? I know we must keep trying to move to stay warm but I'm getting so tired and the icy cold, it makes me want to sleep too, even though I know I must stay awake. I feel my eyes closing.

"Hattie!" Olive jolts, suddenly alert. Ralph stirs. Olive's head turns towards me, our helmets clashing. "Hattie I heard something."

"OMG what is it?" My heartbeat jumps so fast like it's doing a tap dance on my chest. I clutch Ralph's shoulders.

"Probably the Abominable Snowman," Ralph jokes sheepishly before he starts coughing. Is that his way of staying positive?

What if he's right? What if it's not a joke? The cold suddenly feels colder. I've a choking feeling around my throat.

"Seriously listen!" Olive orders.

The wind whistles through the trees, then swoosh. I can hear the occasional sweeping noise.

"There, did you hear that?" she hisses, gripping hold of my arm. Now I'm even more frightened. Darkness is creeping up on us as day turns into night.

"The snowman thing, it was a joke wasn't it?" I check with Ralph.

He doesn't laugh. His teeth are clenched.

The sweeping sound gets closer. I break cover and stand up, spinning around looking for movement in the trees and hold my breath to listen for clues. The storm confuses me, twisters of snow spiraling across the mountain. I can't work out which way the sounds came from. If I see eyes in the woods where will I run to? I can't leave Ralph. Goosebumps tingle down my arms. Olive stumbles over our pile of skis and kit. She grabs a ski pole in each fist, pointing them ahead of her like spears. I jump into action and do the same.

Be warned Abominable Snowman, I am armed!

CHAPTER 29

BLAME

As told by Barney

I'm looking but I don't see you. The darkness is growing thicker. Even the flicker of lights from the snowplough is blurred by the blizzard.

"Talk to me Hattie, give me a sign," I mumble.

"Can you speak to each other in your head, you and Hattie?" Barry quietly asks me as we stand staring out of the window. "Coz you're twins. Are tele…tele…"

He can't remember the word, so Vijay helps him out. "Telepathic."

"Yeah, that's it. Are you telepathic?"

I watch the snowflakes sticking to the window frame, piling up in the corner, and building a mini snowdrift. Every flake is perfect. How can something so fragile fall so far out of the sky and still be perfect? Pressing my nose against the cold glass pane I wonder where Hattie would hide if left out on the mountain. I listen for her voice but she's not speaking.

"Sometimes if she's close by, I can look at Hattie and know what she's thinking."

"Really?" Barry's eyelids open so wide, exposing the whites of his eyes.

I hate to disappoint him. "But I can't speak to Hattie in my head," I admit. I wish I could. I feel so useless sitting here just waiting.

Barry's nose wrinkles. I watch his top lip curl up on one side letting out a puff of air, like a balloon deflating.

"I'm sorry I didn't want to go off piste," he says. "I should've had a go, that way you'd still be with Hattie. Together we'd be strong enough to overpower any horrible snowman." Barry presses his palms together, rubbing his hands up and down. "We'd squash any snowman to the ground. It's my fault. I split the team up." He hangs his head down.

"No mate," I pat my friend on the back, "it's not your fault. Hattie and Olive are the ones who decided to go off piste. Both girls knew it wasn't allowed."

He shrugs.

"They could've caused an avalanche. How selfish is that? If anyone's to blame it's me, I should've stopped Hattie. I tried. I gave her a warning look, you know." I show Barry by frowning and giving my head a shudder rather than a full on shake.

"You did that?" he checks with me. "With the eyes?" He points to my eyebrows drawn together and tries to copy me.

"Yes!" I pause. "But now I think about it, I had my goggles on. Perhaps she couldn't see me properly."

"Well you gave her a chance." My friend makes me feel better.

"She chose to go and so did the others," adds Vijay.

"Yes, they all chose to go," I agree.

Neither of us speaks for a while, as we stand still, staring out of the window, searching for a sign of hope, until Barry breaks the silence.

"Still, I'll never forgive myself if they get eaten."

CHAPTER 30

EYES IN THE WOODS

As told by Hattie

The swishing gets louder. Something is approaching. Olive and I poise ready for battle. Even in pain Ralph manages to grab a pole, holding his arm aloft and waving it threateningly from beneath the fronds. Our heads are fixed up hill towards the noise. I imagine the monster with his thick icy legs thundering through the snow, icicle daggers dangling from his hands and mouth. Icy blue eyes that freeze you on sight. What chance do we have?

We make no sound. I even hold my breath. Still the swishing gets louder.

Can he smell us? How far can he see? I catch a flicker of light that moves so fast it appears to jump from above us over to the trees. Must be its eyes. A monster obviously has night vision.

"Can you see anything?" Ralph hisses.

"No," I growl back.

The noise stops. We freeze. Has it spotted us?

A snapping branch cracks in the woods. A tiny pair of eyes swoops towards us, and I duck hearing the beating of wings. An owl hoots and Olive let's out a squeal.

"What was that?" she exclaims in a high-pitched voice, no longer able remain quiet.

"Just a bird, probably an owl out hunting," I say turning away from the woods. I reach out to give her shoulder a friendly squeeze. She twitches on my touch. "We need a plan," I suggest in a whisper. "In case we're attacked."

"Run!" Olive says.

"Ralph can't run, besides neither can we since we can barely see where we're going. We could stumble off the edge of a cliff."

"You're right, it's too dangerous to run, but you could hide," says Ralph.

"No!" I disagree. "Olive, you and I should stand either side of Ralph to protect him." It feels better to be taking charge.

"We could build a barricade using our skis," Olives suggests and immediately sets to by picking up Ralph's skis and sticking them in the ground at angles so they cross over at the tips. She does the same with my skis on the other side of Ralph.

She looks up at her own skis where she crossed them just after the crash, further up the mountain. Not far, but far enough.

"We need to bring those skis closer," she gulps. Anyone walking out alone would be exposed.

"We'll do it together." I link my arm in hers and we run quickly up the hill, grabbing the skis and retreating. We crouch down next to Ralph behind the barricade.

"You'll have to leave me," Ralph croaks. "If there is a creature, you'll have to leave me. Save yourselves."

"I'm not leaving you," I tell him, my voice is cracking. My lips are dry and chapped and I swallow finding it hard to speak.

Olive appears undecided.

I lean down into the shelter, lift up my goggles off my face and push up the visor on his helmet. Now we can see each other eye to eye, shadowy figures in the fading light. His eyes have lost their sparkle. He must be in so much pain, to know he cannot move, but to offer to be the bait.

"I will not leave you," I state.

"You must. It'll be ok, I'll play dead." He gives me a faint smile.

"You are funny," I smile back.

"Hattie!" Olive gasps.

"What?" I look up to see Olive's wide open mouth. Her face nods from me towards the woods.

"Look at your jacket." She points to the sleeves where the reflective patches light up, and then all goes dark again.

"There's a light coming from the woods," she hisses. I grab my poles and stand ready for action. Like the sweeping beam of a lighthouse, something catches the reflective material on my sleeve again making it glow briefly before the light moves away.

Hypnotised by the swinging light, we watch it cut through the tree trunks. I grip my poles tight and dig my boots into the snow. I'm ready for battle.

"Voices, I hear voices," yelps Olive.

"Are you sure?" I don't hear anything.

"Hello!" Olive shouts. "Help!"

I grab the whistle dangling from my neck and blow three long, loud blasts.

"Wait!" I raise my hand, stopping Olive from shouting again whilst we wait for a reply. I concentrate on listening for a sign but the rustle of the branches blowing in the wind is all I can hear.

"I definitely heard something," Olive assures me. "There!" She pats my arm feverishly.

"I hear it!" voices in the distance. I forget about how cold I feel, the rescuers are near.

"Help!" Olive shouts.

I continue with three blasts on the whistle then Olive and Ralph both yell together.

The noise seems to be getting closer, louder, but then suddenly drifts away.

"Help!" Olive bellows again and so does Ralph.

I reach into the rucksack and pull out the torch. Why didn't I think of this before? Using it as a flashlight, I keep turning it on and off, on and off, shining it in the direction of the voices.

"Help! Help!" Olive's shouts are becoming more frantic now. "What if they miss us and just ski away?" she panics.

"Help! H-E-L-P!" I scream so loud and give a blast on the whistle too.

CHAPTER 31

ABOMINABLE SNOWMAN

As told by Barney

Head bowed and with big glassy eyes looking up at me, magnified by his spectacles, Vijay offers words of wisdom.

"In your time of need Barney, how can I be of help? Ask me anything you like."

Vijay is the font of all knowledge, as Grandpa would say. He's one of those guys who just knows everything, like he's swallowed an encyclopedia. I sit down on the bench beside him.

"Is the Abominable Snowman fact or fiction?" I feel better the minute I ask, like a huge weight has been lifted. If Barry hadn't mentioned the possibility of our friends being eaten, I might not have thought about it. I know it sounds stupid, but it is worrying me, now that my sister and friends are out there, exposed on the mountain. I can guarantee that the minute Ralph first mentioned the Abominable Snowman, Vijay would've gone back that evening and researched it on the web. He's interested in anything that he doesn't already know about.

"Statistically, it's unlikely the Abominable Snowman even exists," he explains. He considers my question very seriously and I appreciate that. "No one has ever seen it."

"That's because people that have seen it were eaten," Barry claims. This isn't helping my nerves.

"But no one has ever found the bones of a human victim," Vijay points out. "The only bones left on the mountain have been animal ones. Animals that could've been eaten by a predator or just died of natural causes."

"What if the horrible snowman eats the human bones?" Barry adds. He's waggling his finger at us. I think he's got something else to say but he can't remember what it is.

"Why would he do that? He'd be at risk of choking," Vijay disagrees.

"There's calcium in them bones. Something as big as the horrible snowman is going to need a lot of calcium. My mum says that's why I need to drink my milk is to keep my big bones healthy."

If this is what being supportive means, I'm no longer finding Barry much use.

My small friend breathes in deeply through his flared nostrils. He is about to speak when… "Oh I do like to be beside the seaside," blasts out of my jacket pocket.

CHAPTER 32

DON'T LEAVE US

As told by Hattie

Lights flickering through the trees are growing in numbers, white beams firing at all angles.

"Don't leave us!" Olive screams.

I jump the barricade and run towards the woods. At the edge of the trees I stand waving my arms, hoping to get the reflective material to shine in the dark, but the lights are already retreating back behind the tree trunks. I wave the torch in my hand, pointing it into the woods. The blizzard swirls around me but I'm not afraid of any ice monster anymore. I can hear people calling out though I can't understand what they are saying.

"Over here! Over here!" I shout. I blow the whistle in a long continuous blast. "We're here!" I'm desperate. Why can't they hear us?

"Help us!" Olive screams but she sounds muffled behind me.

"Help!" Ralph shouts, but the wind is against us. It steals our words, blowing them in the wrong direction.

Suddenly the lights vanish and the voices fall silent. It takes my breath away. There's a pain at the back of my throat.

"No!" I cry out. "Don't leave us!" I shout, panting, trying to gather my breath. Anger is growing like a fire inside me. "Don't leave us!"

Fuelled by rage I run into the still and silent woods. "Wait, wait!" I scream. Twigs snap beneath my boots. I stumble over tree roots, crash through branches, shining the single beam of my torch ahead. Fronds are slapping me in the face as I run. My trousers catch on a sharp branch, ripping through the material and slicing through my skin. "Aarh!"

"Keep going girl, keep going," I repeat like a mantra. My breathing is rapid, there's a burning in my chest. I clasp my belly as I get a stitch. My ski boots feel heavy, like running in concrete shoes. I trip over several times, crashing onto my knees. The wound on my leg stings with every stride. My arms are battling with the thick heavy branches. I dodge and dive through the trees until finally I reach the far side of the small copse, staggering out into the blizzard. I see no one, nothing but falling snow. I fall to my knees blowing hard on my whistle. The cold air cuts my throat as I yell one last time.

PLEASE
HELP US

CHAPTER 33

CONFESSION

As told by Barney

Hattie's shrill ringtone cuts through the hushed chatter in the lounge. I stand up. Everyone's looking at me. My cheeks burn. Goosebumps spread like a rash across my body. Who can be calling?

I pull the phone out. Mum rushes over, grabs it and switches the sounds off. It still vibrates in her hand.

"Aren't you going to answer it?" I ask.

"It's Grandpa," she states, blinking at the screen. "Hattie has a special ringtone for him."

I take the phone back and press the answer button. "Grandpa, hi, it's Barney."

"Hello brilliant Barney, king of the slopes. How's it going?" He sounds so jolly. "I'm just checking in to let you know everything's fine here at home. Clyde the kitten has been behaving, only pooed once in my slippers." This makes me chuckle, instantly forgetting all my worries for a second. "So have you done any daring runs yet?" he asks.

Mum is scratching her head.

"We went down a black run," I tell him. "I mastered it after a few attempts. I only fell over once the last time we went down."

"Put your mind to anything and you can master it Barney." Chatting feels good until he asks, "how did Hattie get on?"

"Uh," I hesitate, "she was good." Actually, Hattie was better than me, her technique was more controlled, but I think that was because she followed Olive, who was mirroring the instructor. Whereas I was near the back most of the time. I remember grumbling about the girls hogging the best positions at the front. Wish I hadn't moaned now.

I realise that Mum is still standing close to me, perhaps listening in to my every word.

"Is she about, shall I say a quick hello?"

"Err, no, Hattie's not here, sh…she's…" I stutter.

Mum cups her hands across her mouth, her eyes begin to weep. I turn away from Mum and walk to a private corner of the lounge.

"Grandpa," I say quietly, desperately thinking how to break the news. "Hattie's in a spot of bother." It sounds like something Grandpa would say himself.

"Oh dear, what's she done?"

I decide to be honest and explain the story right from the start, when Hattie and Olive were plotting to ski alone. I describe how we split into two teams, when the girls went off piste with Ralph. That we were supposed to meet on the blue run. Ski Patrol arrived first but the Dare Devils never showed up and are now missing.

"The thing is, Grandpa," I feel better telling him. "I chose to stay with Barry because really I was scared. I should've gone with her." I fiddle with the zip on my fleece.

There's a pause.

"No Barney, you did the right thing, you stuck with your teammate. I expect Hattie got carried away with the excitement of such a plan and didn't consider all the consequences." His wise words were needed up the mountain to persuade them not to go off piste. "Remember your sister is a clever girl though. She'll work out how to stay safe. You mark my words." He makes everything appear manageable.

"I hope so, but the blizzard is bad," I sigh.

"Shall I speak to your mum quickly, then I'd better get off the phone in case the rescue team try to call."

"OK." I wander back over to where Mum is standing.

"Barney, before you go. I want you to know that you did the right thing, staying with Barry."

"Thanks Grandpa."

CHAPTER 34

SORRY

As told by Hattie

My head falls and waves of tears flood down my cheeks, dripping from my chin and nose. The salty water stings my cracked lips. My vision is blurred with strands of wet hair whipping my face in the chilling blizzard. The white of the snow at night seems to go on forever as if someone poured frothy milk all over the mountains.

"Please don't leave us," I plead, sobbing. "Please."

Gusts of wind howl and wheeze around the valley as if the whole mountain is laughing at me. The orange plastic whistle is dangling from my neck. I sit back on my heels and take hold of it. Grandpa loves the mountains, I think to myself. He'd never give up. He would never give up! My mouth fills with saliva so I spit into the snow. Hot air billows from my nostrils. My eyes burn through the cold air and I throw my head back and scream.

"You won't break me!"

A thunderous echo screeches around me. Then the mountain answers back.

Do I hear voices?

"Hello?"

My head snaps back. I wipe my eyes on my wet gloves, the seams scratching against my skin. The torch still in my hand shines down the mountain.

"Hello?" I hear another man's voice, louder this time.

I stand up and I see a faint light down below. My hands are shaking but I manage to shine my torch in that direction.

"I'm here! Help me!" I blow on the whistle, three short, sharp blasts. "I can hear you!"

The light reflects off my right sleeve. I step into the beam and it lights up my face, blinding me.

"Hattie?"

"Yes! Yes it's Hattie!" I cry as two dark figures make their way towards me.

One man swings his beam off my face and shines it back down the mountain. "She's here!" I hear him shout.

I can't control the shaking and the sobbing as the familiar faces of Eve's brother and Christophe approach me. I collapse into their arms.

"You are safe now Hattie," they tell me. "We are going to take you home."

***

I lead a group of rescuers straight back through the woods.

"Ralph has hurt his leg," I tell his father as he pushes branches aside for me. The tall man's head-torch makes it much easier to see where we are going. "He's in a lot of pain but he's being ever so brave."

"Don't worry, we have all the supplies to look after him," Christophe reassures us. The rest of the group carries the skis and medical supplies through a route they know further up the copse. It's too difficult to drag them through this dense part of the woods.

"Olive! Ralph!" I shout out as we near the far side, "I've found help."

Olive runs over as soon as she sees our light. She greets us at the edge of the woods, hugging me so tightly I can barely breathe.

"Thank you, thank you," she blubs. So relieved, she hugs each one of the rescue team in turn.

Ralph's father races to his side, as does the medic.

"I'm sorry father," I hear Ralph say, sniffing. He's so brave, gulping back his tears. "I know we shouldn't have gone off piste. I'm so sorry."

"You are safe son, that's all that matters." His father's voice is croaky, as he bends to hug his son.

The rescue team reassure us that all will be fine, but we still need to get back to the hotel before we are truly safe. And that means skiing in the dark.

CHAPTER 35

HELLO

As told by Barney

A sparkly case vibrates on the coffee table in the lounge.

Mum lunges, snatching up the phone and swiping it onto speaker. "It's Ralph's father!" she calls out. Everyone rushes to her side to listen. "Hello?"

"Mum," a wobbly, sniffing, tiny voice answers. "It's me, Hattie. Eve's brother found us, they're helping us to get back."

Bizarrely, everybody bursts into floods of tears at the best news you could ever hope to receive.

CHAPTER 36

HEAD TORCH

As told by Hattie

All of the rescue team wear head torches fixed around their helmets, lighting up the scene. After a quick assessment, the medic wraps Ralph's leg in a splint, like a long blow-up armband. Very carefully they transfer him on to banana-boat, a kind of plastic stretcher that slides on the snow. Ralph winces and howls. Olive and I turn our heads.

We collect up our skis and align them next to Christophe. A lady in the team fixes us both up with head torches so that we can see where we are going. Everyone is working so fast. I turn away from the hub of activity, shining my light into the woods. Where once I was scared of what might have been in there watching me, now I just see a winter picture. Snow falling, clinging to the branches of the fir trees that sway in the wind. If we hadn't been found, maybe we would have sheltered amongst the trees until dawn. Nothing looks as scary in daylight.

I'm beginning to shiver. The rush of energy I felt when finding help has left me and shock is taking over.

"Ok, girls, we are ready to go. Let's start skiing and help warm you up," says Christophe. "You need to stay right behind me, do you understand?"

Olive nods.

"What about Ralph?" I ask.

"The team will look after him, they'll be following us," Christophe replies.

Christophe and another one of the rescue team pull away. Olive follows but I hesitate, looking back at Ralph. It was bad enough skiing this in the daylight. I really don't want to ski it in the dark.

"I'll stay right beside you Hattie," Eve's brother reassures me. "It's not far and our head torches will light the way."

I'm reluctant to move but I know I must follow. From deep inside me I summon more courage, and set off with the group into the darkness.

***

It might not be far, but it seems like it takes ages. We go slowly, a few metres at a time for everyone's safety. The rescue team keeps talking to each other and us all the way.

We reach a particularly steep part. Olive halts and will not move, like a horse refusing to jump. "I can't do it!" she begins to freak out, shaking her fists in the air.

"It's OK, it's OK," Christophe is quick to calm her down. He slides alongside her, his skis at right angles to the slope. "We will step down together," he says. "I am here, do not worry. Step beside me."

She takes her first step to the side and locks up against Christophe's ski. "That's it Olive, now bring the other ski down to join it," he encourages her. "It's like a dance Olive, I lead and you follow."

Cautiously, she does exactly what he asks her to do. Gradually their steps down grow wider. All the while he keeps talking to her, and soon Olive reaches the bottom of the steep section without even realizing how far she's gone.

I concentrate on being guided by Eve's brother. I'm struggling, my legs are so tired, but he's an expert guide. No wonder Eve is so good. I wish I had an older brother to look after me.

As we move on, the snow is deep, because of the blizzard. A drop in temperature has frozen the crust of the earlier wet, heavy mush so the fresh snow sits on top making it easier to ski through. We pause regularly to give our weary legs a rest. I can't seem to stop them trembling but the team are patient with Olive and me.

Finally we see the glow of the village in the distance. As we slide across the now gentle slope I start to feel sick and excited all at once. The flashing lights of a snowplough move to greet us, lighting our way back to the bottom of the piste. I can see our hotel clearly now and the crowd of people standing at windows of the hotel lounge.

We drop down onto the piste and ski towards the hotel steps. Mum and Dad run out of the front doors, followed by a woman in a dressing gown with a towel on her head, which is odd.

"Mum, Dad," my voice is hoarse from shouting. My parents swallow me up in their arms before I've even had time to step out of my skis. "I'm so sorry," I weep, tears streaming down my cheeks.

Mum kisses my forehead then leans back and holds my face in her hands. "Don't you ever scare me like that again. Do you hear me?"

"No, I definitely won't, I promise." My whole body is shaking with sobs of relief.

"No off piste until you're as good me," Dad jokes, giving me an extra squeeze. He makes me smile, even if he is embarrassing sometimes.

Their arms are prized apart by small chubby hands.

"Welcome back sis," says Barney. I've never been so pleased to see my twin brother. "I saved you a mug of hot chocolate," he grins, "with extra marshmallows."

CHAPTER 37

WINNING TEAM

As told by Barney

"The initial drop is the worst bit, but after that it's a long smooth slope, I promise." Eve leans over the edge pointing out the route with her pole. "We plop down here and glide all the way to the bottom."

Hmm, easy for her to say. She knows exactly what she's doing, unlike me, who's never done anything like this before. There's even a yellow sign picturing a stick figure skiing downhill with a big black cross through the middle. Surely that's a warning sign? The drop looks deadly.

"We're at the highest point in the resort," Eve continues. "Aren't the views amazing? I reckon they're the best in Austria."

Snow-capped mountains spread for miles ahead, like a world of spiky white meringues. I lean forward as far as I dare without falling. The breeze is chilly, nipping at my nose. This is what it's like to be a bird, high above everything else, floating freely.

"I think I can see Switzerland," claims Barry. "Over there, look there's a flag pole."

"Mmm, maybe," Eve's not sure.

"I'm gonna take a picture to show my mum. She'll never believe that I've been to the top of the world." Barry pulls out his phone and starts lining up his shot.

"He's pointing in the wrong direction," Eve whispers in my ear, but she doesn't make fun of Barry. We let him take the picture; no one else will know the difference, one mountain top looks very similar to another from a distance.

"So are we ready to go?" Eve's brother slides up beside us, towering above me. He balances his ski tips way out over the edge.

"What down there?" I snort.

He flicks one ski, spraying tiny balls of snow off the edge. Some of them roll down the steep cliff gathering more snow as they fall, growing in size. Several crash into an exposed rock face. Splat!

"Yes, off the drop, I've got my kit," he stretches one arm over the opposite shoulder and pats his backpack. "Shall we go for it Barney?"

I shuffle backwards. "What? Are you crazy?"

"But you wanted to be one of the best skiers? You like to win," he reminds me. I quickly look down at the floor, this is embarrassing in front of Eve. I bet she's done this run a thousand times.

Barry sidesteps over to the edge. "That is seriously steep," he whistles. "The Abominable Snowman sleeps somewhere out there."

I frown. I thought we'd agreed that it didn't exist. I watch him assessing the jump, his eyes tracking up and down, his mouth chewing on his tongue.

"You can go if you like Barney," he says poking his phone into a top pocket. "I've got a lunch date to keep with the Secret Assassin, so I'll be going back down in the bucket lift." Barry pushes himself backwards using his poles and proceeds to take his skis off.

"Yeah me too," says Hattie, waving me goodbye as she carries her skis towards the metal cage.

It's our last day skiing and Eve's family have kindly taken us on a tour of some of the places we hadn't yet visited in the resort. Where one mountain ends, another one begins and you seem to be able to ski forever.

Eve, her very tall brother and my mum all wait for my answer.

Mum is biting her bottom lip and her shoulders sag. "Shame your dad didn't come, he would've loved this."

"Dad?" There's no way Dad could tackle anything like this.

"The views are spectacular." She takes a deep breath. "So what are we going to do Barney?"

Eve's brother starts jumping on the spot, eager to go.

"I…, er…," I can feel my shoulders creeping up to my ears lobes as all my muscles tense. Think of something Barney. "We haven't got rucksacks full of gadgets, Mum, we can't possibly go," I suddenly remember. This is my get-out clause. "Or one of those transceiver things."

Tilting her head to one side she checks with me. "Sure you don't want to go anyway? An adventure into the unknown."

Eve's lips are tightly sealed. I wish I could see their eyes, to help me see what they are thinking.

"No, maybe another day." I shake my head and try to act cool. "We'll be late for lunch with all the other families. Dad will wonder where we are, and seeing as Ralph's father's offered to pay for us all, to thank us for the team rescue effort, it'd be rude to arrive late."

"Good point Barney," says Mum pushing her skis away from the edge. "So long as you're sure." I watch her unclip her boots and step out of her skis.

Eve brother's bottom lip sticks out. "What a shame," he sighs loudly, blowing so much air out of his lips that his floppy fringe dances about. Oh no, he's disappointed. He also reverses his skis away from the edge and starts to unclip. My shoulders drop and I feel embarrassed. Eve remains standing on her skis. Her shoulders are shaking. That's when I realise that she is muffling a laugh under her mittens.

"Hang on a minute, what's going on?" Barry and Hattie start to hoot. "Was this a test? Were you all in on it?" I spit. "You were checking whether I'd go off piste weren't you?"

Eve moves across to the lift and starts collecting up her skis. I follow.

Mum is smiling. "Well done Barney, you passed with flying colours."

"I can't believe you all kept this a secret. Is that why we came up here?" I prod Barry and Hattie as we clamber back into the lift. "Whose idea was it?"

"It was a team effort," spouts Hattie. The others nod in agreement. "Team effort, yeah a team effort," they mumble. Eve's brother pats me on the helmet.

"Good answer Barney," he adds. The door of the lift slams shut behind him.

"I would've done it if we had all the right kit and been with a professional," I tell him.

The lift jerks away from the peak and we gently slide down the mountain. Suspended by a thick cable we sail over the top of the rugged wild side and back to the groomed slopes. Barry's filming the journey from our cable car.

"Wow!" Barry coos. "This is like having a drone's view of the slopes. Mum's never seen anything like it. She didn't even step into a lift when we went skiing. In fact, I don't reckon she went any further than the shops."

Hattie is pointing out interesting things for Barry to film. Mum is having a conversation with Eve's family about the new lift system that's been installed to link up several areas. I stand next to Eve at the back of the carriage.

"Have you done that scary route before?" I ask her in a hushed voice. I don't want everyone to listen.

She nods. "Once," she answers modestly. I look down at her leg. I don't mean to, it's not like you can tell or anything as her special limb is hidden under her salopettes. "Even with my bionic leg," she chuckles.

"Sorry, I didn't mean to stare. You're an amazing skier," I blurt out. She blushes, although that could be because we're all squashed together into one carriage like baked beans in a tin.

"Would you like to do that route one day Barney?" she asks quietly. I fiddle with the tops of my poles, deciding what to say. "In the right conditions and with a guide," she suggests. The corner of her lips curl up and she gives me the smallest smile. If only I could see her eyes, I reckon her eyebrows would be raised in hope.

We fly over the top of a piste basher, with its lights flashing. A faint beeping noise can be heard.

I hesitate, then let her down. "Actually, I don't think I'll be ready for a few more years yet. I prefer it on the piste-bashed slopes."

"Yeah, me too," she agrees, her button nose wrinkling as she grins.

***

"That's three times you've won now," Vijay complains. "These cards are rigged."

Eve is beaming as she lays down her winning hand. Ralph keeps passing her his best cards, and so does Hattie. Even Olive leaves a red seven free on the table, open for Eve to play, when I know that Olive's got a black six that she could've played, because I caught a sneaky peek at her cards as she bent forward.

Ralph is lying on the sofa, with his leg in a special boot to fix the break. The girls are fussing over him, fetching drinks and nibbles. It's our last night in the hotel before we go home.

Hattie, Olive and Ralph are all grounded for a month when we get back home. I can't believe my sister didn't argue about it.

Today, however, is all about celebrating being back safe. So here we are on our final evening, all the kids as one team together, playing a mammoth game of cards. Dad has kindly supplied us with hot chocolates covered in mountains of cream, marshmallows and chocolate flakes. Delicious.

I'm glad that Eve's won all the games so far this evening. She deserves it, as she was excellent in the emergency operation. It was Eve that took charge like a team leader and knew exactly what to do. If we'd have left it any longer, the outcome could've been much worse.

That said, this is the final game of our holiday, and I haven't won a single one yet.

"Barney if you can't go, you'll have to pick up," Vijay reminds me.

"Pick up," Olive nudges me, hissing in my ear. "Then Eve will win again," she whispers.

All eyes are on me. I survey my cards. No, I think to myself, no I'm not bowing to peer pressure. I lay down my cards one by one until my hands are empty.

"Yes!" I cry out, giving a little fist pump. "Victory is finally mine."

Eve is laughing at me, along with the others as they throw their cards into the pile. I leave the gang to collect up the pack and wander over to the window.

"Do you think he's out there?" A voice whispers behind me.

I turn to see Ralph, propping himself up on his crutches.

"Who?"

"The Abominable Snowman," he says.

I shrug. Ralph moves forward, so that his nose is nearly touching the window.

"What if he helped the girls by breaking off the branches that they used to shelter me?" Ralph proposes, deadly serious.

"How do you know it's a he?" Hattie appears beside him.

"There was definitely something out there." I swivel to see Olive arrive to join us. "I could feel it watching us," she says thoughtfully.

"The horrible snowman is definitely out there," Barry's hot breath on the back of my head makes me jump. "We heard it Barney didn't we? We heard the moans."

"Maybe it's not so horrible," a bright voice suggests. We all turn to look at Vijay. "Nobody likes being left out, perhaps it wanted to be part of the team."

***

Our cases are packed, ready for an early transfer to the airport in the morning. I lean across to turn the light off and snuggle down under the warm covers.

"Goodnight Barry," I call out to my roommate.

"Night Barney," he replies. We lay in darkness. The wind has dropped, and the mountains are silent. "Barney," my big friend whispers.

"Yeah?"

"Thanks for being my teammate. I won't forget this ski holiday for a long time," he tells me.

"Me neither," I reply.

"It's been FRANKTASTIC!" he booms.

"FRANKtastic!"®

THE END

Have you read?

If you enjoy the books,

share them with a friend.

9 781999 711177